RTF
Pocket Guide

D1471533

Sean M. Burke

O'REILLY®

Beijing · Cambridge · Farnham · Köln · Paris · Sebastopol · Taipei · Tokyo

RTF Pocket Guide
by Sean M. Burke

Copyright © 2003 O'Reilly & Associates, Inc. All rights reserved.
Printed in the United States of America.

Published by O'Reilly & Associates, Inc., 1005 Gravenstein Highway North, Sebastopol, CA 95472.

O'Reilly & Associates books may be purchased for educational, business, or sales promotional use. Online editions are also available for most titles (*safari.oreilly.com*). For more information, contact our corporate/institutional sales department: (800) 998-9938 or *corporate@oreilly.com*.

Editor:	Linda Mui
Production Editor:	Colleen Gorman
Cover Designer:	Ellie Volckhausen
Interior Designer:	David Futato

Printing History:

July 2003:   First Edition.

0-596-00475-3
[C]   [9/03]

Contents

Part III. Example Programs

Part IV. Reference Tables

RTF Tutorial

This book is a convenient reference for Rich Text Format (RTF). It covers the essentials of RTF, especially the parts that you need to know if you're writing a program to generate RTF files. This book is also a useful introduction to parsing RTF, although that is a more complex task.

RTF is a document format. RTF is not intended to be a markup language anyone would use for coding entire documents by hand (although it has been done!). Instead, it's meant to be a format for document data that all sorts of programs can read and write. For example, if you even just skim this book, you should be able to write a program (in the programming language of your choice) that can analyze the contents of a database and produce a summary of it as an RTF document with whatever kinds of formatting you want. The flexibility of RTF makes it an ideal format for everything from generating invoices or sales reports, to producing dictionaries based on databases of words.

This book is *not* a complete reference to every last feature of RTF; Microsoft's comprehensive but terse *Rich Text Format (RTF) Specification* is the closest you will find to that. The current version (v1.7) is available at *http://msdn.microsoft. com/library/en-us/dnrtfspec/html/rtfspec.asp*. In the Microsoft Knowledgebase at *support.microsoft.com*, its access number is 269575. Version 1.5 of the specification and before are more verbose, and might be more useful. Microsoft doesn't distribute copies of them anymore, but you can find them all over the Internet by running a search on "Rich Text Format (RTF) Specification" in Google or a similar search engine.

Why RTF?

RTF is a handy format for several reasons.

RTF is a mature format.   RTF's syntax is stable and straightforward, and its specification has existed for over a decade—an eternity in computer years. In fact, while there has been a proliferation of incompatible binary formats calling themselves "Microsoft Word file format," RTF has stayed the course and evolved along backward-compatible lines. That means if you generate an RTF file today, you should be able to read it in 10 years, and you should have no trouble reading an RTF file generated 10 years ago.

Many applications understand RTF.   Since RTF has been around for so long, just about every word processor since the late 1980s can understand it. While not every word processor understands every RTF feature perfectly, most of them understand the RTF commands discussed in this book quite well. Moreover, RTF is the data format for "rich text controls" in MSWindows APIs; RTF-rendering APIs are part of the Carbon/Cocoa APIs in Mac OS X; and you can even read RTF documents on iPods, Apple's portable music players.

Most people have the software to read RTF.   That is, if you email an RTF file to a dozen people you know, chances are that almost all of them can read it with a word processor already on their system, whether it's MSWord, some other word processor (ABIWord, StarOffice, TextEdit), or just the RTF-literate *write.exe* that has been part of MSWindows since at least Windows 98.

In RTF, format control is straightforward.   In HTML, if you want to control the size and style of text or the positioning and justification of paragraphs, the best you can do is try a long detour through CSS, a standard that is erratically implemented even today. In RTF, font size and style, paragraph indenting, page breaks, page numbering, page headers and footers, widow-and-orphan control, and dozens of other features are each a single, simple command.

RTF is a multilingual format.   RTF now supports Unicode, so it can represent text in just about every human language ever written.

RTF is easy to generate.   You can produce RTF without any knowledge of the font metrics needed for Adobe Post-Script or PDF. In addition, since RTF files are text files, it's easy to produce RTF with a program in any programming language, whether it's Perl, Java, C++, Pascal, COBOL, Lisp, or anything in between.

This Book's Approach

This book does not discuss the task of parsing RTF documents. RTF is like many other formats, in that when you want to output in that format, you can stick to whatever syntactic and semantic subset of the language is most convenient for you. But in parsing, you have to be able to accept anything you're given, which may use every last syntactic and semantic oddity mentioned in the spec, and many more that aren't in the spec.

This book explains the simplest kind of RTF, which should work with just about any RTF-aware application. However, I may refer to less-portable commands when necessary, or demonstrate solving a specific problem with an RTF command that also has a broader, more abstract meaning that I do not discuss, for reasons of brevity. If you are particularly interested in the deeper complexities of RTF or of any particular command, you can read this book as a friendly introduction to RTF, and then read the RTF Specification and maybe even view raw RTF code generated by a few different word processors. But for most programmers, this book is more or less everything you'd ever want to know about RTF.

Here's a quick rundown of what you'll find in this book:

Part I, *RTF Tutorial*
Part I teaches RTF to the uninitiated. It explains the basic formatting commands and how to work with them.

Part II, *Creating MS Windows Help Files*
Part II is about creating help files for Microsoft Windows with RTF.

Part III, *Example Programs*
Part III shows several programming examples in RTF, using the Perl programming language.

Part IV, *Reference Tables*
Part IV is the reference section of the book. It includes a character chart, a listing of the language codes, and a conversion table for twips measurements. For more help with measurements, see the twips ruler on the inside of this book's back cover.

RTF "Hello, World!"

The first program you ever learned to write probably looked like this:

```
10 PRINT "HELLO, WORLD!"
```

Even though RTF is a document language instead of a programming language, I'll start out the same. Here is a minimal RTF document:

```
{\rtf1\ansi\deff0 {\fonttbl {\f0 Times New Roman;}}
\f0\fs60 Hello, World!
}
```

If you open a text editor, type that in, save it as *test.rtf*, and then open it with a word processor, it will show you a document consisting of the words "Hello, World!". Moreover, they'll be in the font Times New Roman, in 30-point type.

(We'll go over these commands later, but you may wonder about \fs60 meaning 30 points—it so happens that the parameter for the font-size command is in half-points.) If you wanted them to be in 14-point Monotype Corsiva, change the document to read like this:

```
{\rtf1\ansi\deff0 {\fonttbl {\f0 Monotype Corsiva;}}
\f0\fs28 Hello, World!
}
```

If you want the text to be 60-point, italic, bold, and centered, and to have each word on its own line, do it like this:

```
{\rtf1\ansi\deff0 {\fonttbl {\f0 Monotype Corsiva;}}
\qc\f0\fs120\i\b Hello,\line World!
}
```

Viewed in an MSWord window, that document looks like Figure 1.

Figure 1. "Hello, World!" document viewed in MSWord

You can get exactly the same document if you remove all the newlines in your RTF, like so (because you're reading this in hardcopy instead of on a monitor, I had to break the line, but pretend I didn't):

```
{\rtf1\ansi\deff0{\fonttbl{\f0 Monotype Corsiva;
}}\qc\f0\fs120\i\b Hello,\line World!}
```

Or you can insert many newlines, in certain places:

```
{\rtf1\ansi\deff0
{\fonttbl
{\f0
Monotype Corsiva;
}
}
\qc
\f0\fs120\i
\b Hello,
\line
World!
}
```

Or you can insert just one or two newlines, but insert a space after each *foo* command, like so:

```
{\rtf1 \ansi \deff0 {\fonttbl {\f0 Monotype Corsiva;}}
\qc \f0 \fs120 \i
\b Hello,\line World!}
```

All these syntaxes mean exactly the same thing. However, this doesn't mean that RTF ignores all whitespace the way many computer languages do. I explain the rules for RTF syntax later, in the section "Basic RTF Syntax," so that you'll know when it's okay to add whitespace.

Overview of Simple RTF

Suppose that instead of "Hello, World!", you want something more classy—in fact, more classical. Suppose you want to say hello in Latin. Latin for "Hello, World!" is "Salvête, Omnês!" The question is, how do you get those "ê" characters? You can't just insert a literal "ê" into the RTF document; although a few word processors tolerate that, by-the-book RTF is limited to newline plus the characters between ASCII 32 (space) and ASCII 126 (the "~" character)—and "ê" is not in that range.

But ê is in the ANSI character set (also known as Code Page 1252, which is basically Latin-1 with some characters added between 128 and 159). An extended ASCII chart shows that ê is character 234 in those character sets. To express that

---

character in RTF, use the escape sequence \'*xy*, in which you replace *xy* with the two-digit hexadecimal representation of that character's number. Since 234 in hexadecimal is "ea" (14 * 16 + 10), ê is \'ea in RTF. The Latin phrase "Salvête, Omnês!" is expressed like this:

```
{\rtf1\ansi\deff0 {\fonttbl {\f0 Monotype Corsiva;}}
\qc\f0\fs120\i\b Salv\'eate,\line Omn\'eas!}
```

Figure 2 shows how it looks in MSWord.

Figure 2. "Hello, World!", the Latin version

A text full of \'*xy* codes can make RTF source unreadable, but RTF was never designed with readability as a goal.

The ASCII character chart in Part IV is a table of characters along with the \'*xy* code that you need to reference each one. For Unicode characters (i.e., characters over 255), you can't use a \'*xy* code, since the codes for those characters don't fit in two hex digits. Instead, there's another sequence for Unicode characters, as explained in the section "Character Formatting."

Now, when you see this chunk of RTF code:

```
{\rtf1\ansi\deff0 {\fonttbl {\f0 Monotype Corsiva;}}
\qc\f0\fs120\i\b Salv\'eate,\line Omn\'eas!}
```

you may wonder what each bit means. Commands are discussed in detail later, but to give you just a taste of how RTF works, the following is a token-by-token explanation. You don't need to remember any of the codes mentioned here, as they will be properly introduced later.

The {\rtf1 at the start of the file means "the file that starts here will be in RTF, Version 1," and it is required of all RTF documents. (It so happens that there is no RTF Version 0, nor is there likely to be an RTF Version 2 because the current version's syntax is extensible as it is.) The \ansi means that this document is in the ANSI character set (that is, normal Windows Code Page 1252).* Without this declaration, a reader wouldn't know what character set to use in resolving \'*xy* sequences.

The \deff0 says that the default font for the document is font #0 in the font table, which immediately follows. The {\fonttbl...} construct is for listing the names of all the fonts that may be used in the document, associating a number with each. The {\fonttbl...} construct contains a number of {\f*number fontname*;} constructs, for associating a number with a fontname. This ends the prolog to the RTF document; everything afterward is actual text.

The \qc, the first part of the actual text of the document, means that this paragraph should be centered. (It can be inferred that the "c" in \qc is for *center*, but it would surprise me if most users knew that the "q" is for *quadding*, a now rarely-used term for how to justify the paragraph. Normally there are mnemonics for the commands, but they occasionally become obscure.) The \f0 means that we should now use the font that in the font table we associated with the number 0, namely, Monotype Corsiva. The \fs120 means to

---

* Some old Macintosh word processors wrongly ignore the \ansi declaration and incorrectly resolve character numbers as MacAscii, so that \'ea comes out not as "ê" (character number hex-EA in the ANSI character set), but instead as "á", since that's the character number hex-EA in MacAscii.

change the font size to 60 point. As mentioned earlier, the \fs command's parameter is in half-points: so \fs120 means 60pt, \fs26 means 13pt, and \fs15 means 7½pt.

As you probably inferred, \i means italic, and \b means bold. The space after the \b doesn't actually appear in the text, but merely ends the \b token.

The literal text Salv\'eate, (including the comma) is just "Salvête," with the ê escaped. The command \line means to start a new line within the current paragraph, just like a <BR> in HTML does. Then we have the literal text Omn\'eas!, which is just "Omnês!" escaped. And finally, we end the document with a }. While there are other }'s in the document, we know that it is the one that ends this document because it matches the { that started the document, and because there is nothing after it in this file. Unless an RTF file ends with a } that matches the leading {, it's an error, and errors are treated unpredictably by different RTF-reading applications.

Basic RTF Syntax

So far we've taken an informal view of RTF syntax. But to go any further, we'll need to explain it in more careful terms, considering the kinds of syntactic tokens that exist in the RTF language, and their range of meanings.

RTF breaks down into four basic categories: commands, escapes, groups, and plaintext.

An RTF *command* is like \pard or \fs120: a backslash, some lowercase letters, maybe an integer (which might have a negative sign before it), and then maybe a single meaningless space character. In terms of regular expressions, a command matches /\\[a-z]+(-?[0-9]+)? ?/ (including the optional space at the end). An RTF parser knows that a command has ended when it sees a character that no longer matches that pattern. For example, an RTF parser knows that \i\b is two commands because the second "\" couldn't possibly be a

Syntax Errors

When an application sees a syntax error in RTF, it might:

- Reject the file entirely; for example, MSWord 2000 aborts when reading malformed RTF files and confusingly reports "The document name or path is not valid."
- Abort reading but leave the document text, up to the error.
- Ignore the error and keep reading; or it might infer that this is not actually an RTF file, and re-read it as a plain-text file.
- Crash.

Over the years, I've seen all these things happen as different applications try reading malformed RTF files. The lesson is that applications aren't forgiving of syntax errors in RTF.

Mercifully, just about the only real syntax error you are likely to make is in not having your {'s and }'s balanced—something that you can find easily with an editor's "balance" feature (on the "%" key in *vi*, or the "meta-(" key sequence in *emacs*). Just about every other kind of error, like misspelling a command name, will typically not be treated as a syntax error to an RTF-reading application.

For example, if you misspell the center-paragraph command \qc as \cq, the RTF-reading application parses it as a perfectly valid command. The fact that there is no actual "cq" command in RTF means that the application would just ignore it.

continuation of the \i command. For another example, in \pard*, the * couldn't possibly be a continuation of the \pard command, because an asterisk can't be part of a command name, nor could it even be part of the optional integer; and of course it can't be the optional meaningless space.

RTF *escapes* are like commands in that they start with a backslash, but that's where the similarity ends. The character after the backslash is *not* a letter. If the escape is \' then the next two characters will be interpreted as hex digits, and the escape is understood to mean the character whose ASCII code is the given hex number. For example, the escape `\'ea` means the ê character, because character 0xEA in ASCII is ê. But if the character after the \ isn't an apostrophe, the escape consists of just that one character.

There are only three escapes that are of general interest: `\~` is the escape that indicates a nonbreaking space; `\-` is an optional hyphen (a.k.a. a *hyphenation point*); and `\_` is a non-breaking hyphen (that is, a hyphen that that's not safe for breaking the line after). The escape `\*` is also part of a construct discussed later. Be sure to note that there is no optional meaningless space after escapes; while `\foo\bar` is the same as `\foo \bar`, `\'ea\'ea` means something different than `\'ea \'ea`. The first one means "êê" (no space) and the second one means "ê ê" (with a space).

An RTF *group* is whatever is between a { and the matching }. For example, `{\i Hi there!}` is a group that contains the command `\i` and the literal text `Hi there!`. Some groups are only necessary for certain constructs (like the `{\fonttbl...}` construct we saw earlier). But most groups have a more concrete purpose: to act as a barrier to the effects of character formatting commands. If you want to italicize the middle word in "a sake cup", use the code `a {\i sake} cup`. In terms of how this is parsed, the { means "save all the character formatting attributes now," and the } means "restore the character formatting attributes to their most recently saved values."

The idea of a group in RTF is analogous to the idea of blocks in "Algol-like" or "block-structured" languages such as C, Perl, Pascal, modern Basic dialects, and so forth; if you are familiar with the idea of "block scope" in such languages, you should be at home with the notion of groups in RTF.

It's tempting to view code like `{\i...}` as just the RTF way to express what HTML or XML express with `<i>...</i>`. This is a useful way to look at it, but it doesn't explain RTF code like `{a \i sake} cup`, which in fact means the same thing as `a {\i sake} cup`.

The final bit of RTF syntax is *plaintext*: the text that is sent right through to the document, character for character. For example, when we had Hello, World! in our document, it turned into the text that said simply "Hello, World!".

Newlines and Spaces in RTF

Many computer languages don't distinguish between different kinds of whitespace. So, for example, in the PostScript graphics language, the code newpath 300 400 100 0 180 arc fill draws a black half-circle in about the middle of the page. You could write that code compactly on one line:

```
newpath 300 400 100 0 180 arc fill
```

Or in place of the spaces there, you could insert any mix of spaces, newlines, and tabs:

```
newpath
   300   400
   100   0
     180
          arc
  fill
```

Similarly, in Lisp, these two bits of code mean the same thing:

```
(while (search-forward "x" nil t) (replace-match "X" t t))

(while
  (
    search-forward  "x"  nil  t
  )
  (replace-match "X" t t)
)
```

And in HTML, these are the same:

```
<b>Get me a cup of <i>sake</i>, okay?<b>

<b>Get
  me    a      cup
        of <i>sake</i>,
    okay?<b>
```

However, RTF is not that kind of language. In RTF, the rules for dealing with whitespace are very different:

- A space character is meaningless *only* if it's the optional meaningless space at the end of a command. Otherwise, every space character means to insert a space character!
- A newline can mark the end of the command; but otherwise, it has no effect or meaning.

For example, consider in{\i cred}ible, in which the space ends the \i command, but doesn't actually add a space to the document. In all other cases, a space in the source means a space in the document. For example:

```
Space,     the {\b
final frontier}
```

Here, there are five spaces after the comma, and they really do insert five spaces into the document. Also, the newline after \b marks the end of the \b command. If that newline were removed, the code would look like \bfinal frontier, which the parser would interpret as a command called \bfinal (plus a meaningless space that ends the command) and then the word frontier.

A newline (or 2 or 15) doesn't indicated a linebreak. For example, this code:

```
in
cred

ible
```

Means the same as this:

```
incredible
```

This may seem a very strange way for a markup language to go about doing things. But RTF isn't really a markup language; it's a data format that happens to be used for expressing text documents. It was never meant to be something that people would find easy and intuitive for typing. Nor is machine-generated RTF typically easy for people to read. However, when you write RTF-generating programs, try to produce easy-to-read source, since it makes programs easier to debug.

Your programs should insert a newline for two reasons: first, in order to make logical divisions in the RTF source; second, to avoid lines that are overly long (like over 250 characters), which become unwieldy to look at in many editors, and occasionally cause trouble when transferred through email. Here are some rules of thumb for putting linebreaks in RTF:

- Put a newline before every \pard or \par (commands that are explained in the "Paragraphs" section).

- Put a newline before and after the RTF font-table, stylesheet, and other similar constructs (like the optional color table, described later).

- You can put a newline after every *N*th space, {, or }. (Alternately: put a newline after every space, {, or } that's after the 60th column.)

As you're massaging RTF source, consider avoiding having the word "From" occur at the start of a line—either break the line elsewhere, or represent it as \'46rom. Email protocols occasionally turn "From" at line start into ">From" even in text-encoded attachments like RTF files. Escaping the "F" keeps that from happening.

Paragraphs

This is the basic construct for a paragraph in RTF:

```
{\pard ... \par}
```

For example, consider this document of 2 plain paragraphs in 12pt Times:

```
{\rtf1\ansi\deff0 {\fonttbl {\f0 Times;}}\fs24

{\pard
Urbem Romam a principio reges habuere; libertatem et
consulatum L. Brutus instituit. dictaturae ad tempus
sumebantur; neque decemviralis potestas ultra biennium,
neque tribunorum militum consulare ius diu valuit.
\par}

{\pard
```

```
Non Cinnae, non Sullae longa dominatio; et Pompei Crassique potentia
cito in Caesarem, Lepidi atque Antonii arma in Augustum cessere, qui
cuncta discordiis civilibus fessa nomine principis sub imperium
accepit.
\par}
}
```

Formatted, they look like Figure 3.

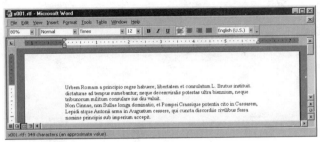

Figure 3. Two plain paragraphs

The RTF idea of "paragraph" is broader than what you're
probably used to. We might call whatever HTML implements with a <p> tag a paragraph, but the RTF concept of
"paragraph" corresponds to almost everything in HTML that
isn't a character-formatting tag such as .... For
example, what we would call a heading is implemented in
RTF as just a (generally) short paragraph with (generally)
large type. For example, consider the heading "Annalium
Romae" in the following RTF (which appears formatted in
Figure 4):

```
{\rtf1\ansi\deff0 {\fonttbl {\f0 Times;}}
\fs24
{\pard \fs44 Annalium Romae\par}
{\pard
Urbem Romam a principio reges habuere; libertatem et
consulatum L. Brutus instituit. dictaturae ad tempus
sumebantur; neque decemviralis potestas ultra biennium,
neque tribunorum militum consulare ius diu valuit.
\par}
{\pard
```

```
Non Cinnae, non Sullae longa dominatio; et Pompei Crassique potentia
cito in Caesarem, Lepidi atque Antonii arma in Augustum cessere, qui
cuncta discordiis civilibus fessa nomine principis sub imperium
accepit.
\par}
}
```

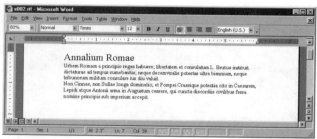

Figure 4. A heading

Right after the \pard in each paragraph, you can add commands that control the look of that paragraph. There are several kinds of paragraph-formatting commands, and we will
go through them in groups.

A word of warning: if you're at home with very "semantic"
markup languages like LaTeX or XML-based document languages, you may be be taken aback by the idea that RTF
treats headings as a kind of paragraph—don't headings and
paragraphs *mean* different things? RTF takes a different
approach: RTF is about how things look. RTF doesn't care
about the semantic difference between italics for emphasis
(You said *what?*) versus italics for titles (*Naked Lunch*) versus italics for names of ships (*Lusitania*)—to RTF it's all just
italics. Of course, if you do want to add a layer of semantic
tagging to RTF documents, you can use styles (covered later
in this part of the book); but even then, RTF is still about
appearances, because RTF styles don't replace appearances,
they just add to them.

About {\pard ... \par}

Since {\pard...\par} is such a common construct, it must be explained that its parts do have independent meanings. The \pard means to reset the paragraph-formatting attributes to their default value, instead of inheriting them (or some of them!) from the previous paragraph. The \par means to end the current paragraph. The {...} around the whole construct isn't totally necessary, but it keeps font changes from spilling into subsequent paragraphs. While a \par or a \pard could each exist on their own, and could exist outside of a surrounding {...} group, I have found that this makes for RTF code that is very hard to debug. My experience has been that {\pard...\par} is the sanest and safest way to express paragraphs.

In an ideal world, the construct for paragraphs would be something like {\p...}. Hindsight is 20/20. We have to make do with having a \pard command to start, and a command \par to end. Luckily, command-pairs like that are relatively rare in RTF.

Controlling Paragraph Justification and Centering

The first commands we will cover are ones that tell the word processor how to *justify* the lines on in the current paragraph—namely, whether to make the lines flush on the left margin, or the right, or both, or whether to center each line.

\ql
> Left-justify this paragraph (leave the right side ragged). This is generally the default.

\qr
> Right-justify this paragraph (leave the left side ragged). This is rarely used.

`\qj`

Full-justify this paragraph (try to make both sides smooth).

`\qc`

Center this paragraph. This is generally used only for headings, not normal paragraphs. Each line of the heading/paragraph is centered.

The following RTF code is an example that demonstrates centering, full justification, and left-justification. It is shown formatted in Figure 5.

```
{\rtf1\ansi\deff0 {\fonttbl {\f0 Times;}}
\fs34
{\pard \qc \fs60 Annalium Romae\par}
{\pard \qj
Urbem Romam a principio reges habuere; libertatem et
consulatum L. Brutus instituit. dictaturae ad tempus
sumebantur; neque decemviralis potestas ultra biennium,
neque tribunorum militum consulare ius diu valuit.
\par}
{\pard \ql
Non Cinnae, non Sullae longa dominatio; et Pompei Crassique potentia
cito in Caesarem, Lepidi atque Antonii arma in Augustum cessere, qui
cuncta discordiis civilibus fessa nomine principis sub imperium
accepit.
\par}
```

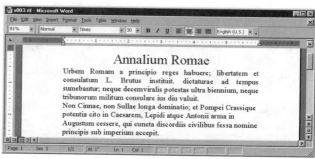

Figure 5. Centering, full justification, and left-justification

Spacing Between Paragraphs

There are two simple commands for adding space over and under the current paragraph: \sb and \sa, for space before and space after. But take note: they don't measure the space in centimeters or pixels or inches or anything else familiar. Instead, the space is measured in *twips*, a unit that RTF uses for almost everything. A twip is a 1,440th of an inch, or about a 57th of a millimeter. The name *twip* comes from a twentieth of a point (a *point* is a typesetting unit here defined as a 72nd of an inch). Points are rarely used except for expressing the size of a font. To help you measure distances in twips, the section "Converting to Twips" in Part IV shows conversions between twips and inches and centimeters. Also, see the twips ruler inside the back cover of this book.

\sbN

> Add N twips of (vertical) space before this paragraph. By default, this is 0. For example, \sb180 adds 180 twips (an eighth of an inch) before this paragraph.

\saN

> Add N twips of (vertical) space after this paragraph. By default, this is 0. For example, \sb180 adds 180 twips (an eighth of an inch) after this paragraph.

Generally, the effect you are after is space between paragraphs, and the simplest way to create it is to give every paragraph a \sa command. (If you had an \sb on each one, then the first paragraph on the first page would have some space before it, and it would look odd.)

For example, taking the RTF source that gave us Figure 4 and changing every paragraph to start out with {\pard\sa180 gives Figure 6's formatting, which nicely separates the paragraphs visually.

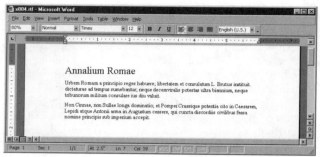

Figure 6. Space added between paragraphs

Paragraph Indenting

There are three paragraph-formatting commands that control *indenting*, in various ways:

\fiN

> Indent the first line of this paragraph by *N* twips. For example, \fi720 will indent the first line by 720 twips (a half-inch). This is the common sense of the English word "indent." But you can also use a negative number to "outdent"—i.e., to have the first line start further to the *left* than the rest of the paragraph, as with \fi-720.

\liN

> This command and the following command control *block indenting*, i.e., indenting not just the first line, but the whole paragraph. The \liN command expresses how far in from the left margin this paragraph should be block-indented.

\riN

> This command sets how far in from the right margin this paragraph should be block-indented.

Note that \fi doesn't start indenting from the left margin of the page, but from the left margin of the paragraph (which \li may have set to something other than the left page-margin).

For example, consider the three paragraphs in Figure 7, the first of which starts out with {\pard \fi720 \qj\sa180, the second with {\pard \fi-1440 \li2800 \qj\sa180, and the third with {\pard \li2160 \ri2160 \qj\sa180.

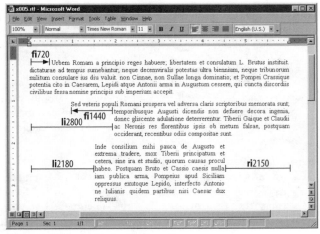

Figure 7. Different kinds of indentation

Bear in mind that the left and right margin do not mean the left and right edge of the page; typically, the margins are an inch in from the edge of the page. For more about changing the margins, see the "Page Margins" section later.

Paragraphs and Pagebreaks

There are seven commands that control how the pagebreaking and linebreaking settings interact with paragraphs:

\pagebb

Make this paragraph start a new page, i.e., put a pagebreak before this paragraph.

\keep

Try to not split this paragraph across pages, i.e., keep it in one piece.

\keepn

Try to avoid a pagebreak between this paragraph and the next—i.e., keep this paragraph with the next one. This command is often used on headings, to keep them together with the following text paragraph.

\widctlpar

Turn on widow-and-orphans control for this paragraph. This is a feature that tries to avoid breaking a paragraph between its first and second lines, or between its second-to-last and last lines, since breaking in either place looks awkward. Since you'd normally want this on for the whole document, not just for a particular paragraph, you probably want to just use a single \widowctrl command at the start of the document, as discussed in the "Preliminaries" section.

\nowidctlpar

Turn off widow-and-orphans control for this paragraph. This is useful when \widowctrl has turned on widows-and-orphans control for the whole document but you want to disable it for just this paragraph.

\hyphpar

This turns on automatic hyphenation for this paragraph. Since you normally want this on for the whole document, you probably want to just use a single \hyphauto at the start of the document, as discussed in "Preliminaries."

\hyphpar0

This command turns off automatic hyphenation for this paragraph. This is a useful when you have a \hyphauto set for this document, but you want to exempt a few paragraphs from hyphenation. (Technically, \hyphpar0 isn't a separate command—it's just a \hyphpar command with a parameter value of 0.)

For example, the code below makes a heading that shouldn't be split up from the following paragraph, and then makes that paragraph, which consists of several lines of verse that shouldn't be broken across pages. Figure 8 shows the result.

```
{\pard \fs60 \keepn \qc .IX.\par}
{\pard \keep
Nullus in urbe fuit tota qui tangere vellet\line
   uxorem gratis, Caeciliane, tuam,\line
dum licuit: sed nunc positis custodibus ingens\line
   turba fututorum est: ingeniosus homo es.
\par}
```

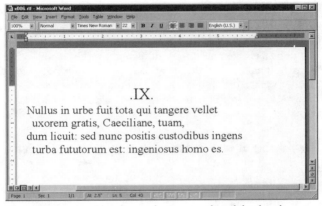

Figure 8. A centered heading and a paragraph with linebreaks

Double-Spacing

To double-space a paragraph, put the code \sl480\slmult1 right after the \pard. To triple-space it, use \sl720\slmult1. To have just 1.5-spacing, use \sl360\slmult1. A single-spaced paragraph is the default, and doesn't need any particular code. (The magic numbers 480, 720, and 360 don't depend on the point size of the text in the paragraph.)

You might think it's a limitation that line-spacing is an attribute of paragraphs. For example, in WordPerfect, the internal code for line-spacing can be set anywhere in any paragraph—it takes effect starting on that line, and can last for the rest of the document. Whereas with RTF's way of doing things, you can only set line-spacing (and many other features) for a paragraph, and the settings don't automatically apply to the following paragraphs. Why does RTF do it that way? Basically, because MSWord does it that way, and the designers of RTF tended to model it after the internal format of MSWord documents.

Exact Paragraph Positioning

Paragraphs are usually placed below the previous one and against the left margin. However, in some cases, such as when printing labels, you need to print text at a specific spot on the page. In that case, use the \pvpg\phpg\posx$X$\posy$Y$\absw$W$ construct to place the start of the paragraph X twips across and Y twips down from the top left of the page, with a width of W twips. That construct goes after the \pard at the start of a paragraph.

For example, the following paragraph is positioned with the top-left tip of its first letter (the "U" in "Urbem") 2,160 twips left and 3,600 twips down from the top-left corner of the page. The paragraph will be 4,320 twips wide:

```
{\pard \pvpg\phpg \posx2160 \posy3600 \absw4320
Urbem Romam a principio reges habuere; libertatem et
  consulatum L. Brutus instituit. dictaturae ad tempus
  sumebantur; neque decemviralis potestas ultra biennium,
\par}
```

You can put a border around this paragraph by adding a rather large block of commands after the \pard:

```
\brdrt \brdrs \brdrw10 \brsp20
\brdrl \brdrs \brdrw10 \brsp80
\brdrb \brdrs \brdrw10 \brsp20
\brdrr \brdrs \brdrw10 \brsp80
```

Normally, the paragraph (and any border around it) extends just as far down as the paragraph needs in order to show all its lines. However, you can add a \absh$MinHeight$ command after the \absw, to force the paragraph to be at least $MinHeight$ twips high; the word processor will format this by adding space to the bottom of the paragraph if it would otherwise come out at shorter than *MinHeight* twips high. If you have borders on this paragraph, any added space will be between the bottom of the paragraph and the bottom border (instead of just being under the bottom border).

Or you can use the \absh-*ExactHeight* command to set the exact height of the paragraph (and any borders). For example, the following paragraph will be inside a box (created by the border lines) 5,760 twips high:

```
{\pard \pvpg\phpg \posx2160 \posy3600 \absw4320
\absh-5760
\brdrt \brdrs \brdrw10 \brsp20
\brdrl \brdrs \brdrw10 \brsp80
\brdrb \brdrs \brdrw10 \brsp20
\brdrr \brdrs \brdrw10 \brsp80
Urbem Romam a principio reges habuere; libertatem et
  consulatum L. Brutus instituit. dictaturae ad tempus
  sumebantur; neque decemviralis potestas ultra biennium,
\par}
```

If the current font and point size makes the text take up only a part of the space in that box, then there is just blank space left at the bottom. But if the text is too large to fit in that box, the extra text is hidden. That is, only as much of the paragraph is shown as actually fits in that box, because of the \absh-*ExactHeight* command.

The only syntactic difference between the \absh*MinHeight* command and the \absh-*ExactHeight* command is the negative sign. This is indeed an unusual use of the negative sign, since it uses -*N* to mean something very different from *N*, whereas you would expect -*N* to mean simple "*N*, but in the other direction."

The full set of commands for exact positioning are explained in the "Positioned Objects and Frames" section of the RTF specification. The border commands are explained in the "Paragraph Borders" section of the RTF specification. We will also see a very similar construct for table cell borders in the "Preliminaries" section of this book.

Character Formatting

The RTF commands in the previous chapter (\keepn, \qc, etc.) influence the layout of text, not the size and style of the text itself. To change the size and style, we use character formatting commands, almost always in combination with {...} groups. For example, \i turns on italics, but we wouldn't be easily able to use it in combination with non-italic text unless we used it as {\i...}, in which the first { means to save the current character formatting that's in effect before the \i takes effect, and then the } restores that formatting. Using the example from our discussion of syntax in "Basic RTF Syntax," here's how we set the word "sake" in italics in the text "a sake cup":

```
... a {\i sake} cup ...
```

If not for that {...}, the \i would turn on italics and it would probably stay on until the end of the current paragraph.

Basic Character Formatting

Here's a list of the basic character formatting commands:

\i

Italics: "I saw *Brazil* yesterday."

```
I saw {\i Brazil} yesterday.
```

\b

Boldface: "The director's cut is **much** better."

```
The director's cut is {\b much} better.
```

\ul

Underlining: "I even have the <u>script</u> for it."

```
I even have the {\ul script} for it.
```

\super

Superscript: "I'll lend you it on the 5th."

```
I'll lend you it on the 5{\super th}.
```

`\sub`

> Subscript: "Just don't get any H_2O on it, okay?"

```
Just don't get any H{\sub 2}O on it, okay?
```

`\scaps`

> Smallcaps: "Or I'll have the CIA come mess you up!"

```
Or I'll have the {\scaps cia} come mess you up!
```

`\strike`

> Strikethrough: "Because you're a ~~communist~~terrorist!"

```
Because you're a {\strike communist}terrorist!
```

Font Commands

To change the font or the font size, we can't use a simple command (as with `\i` or the like); instead we need a command with a number after it. The command `\fsN` changes the font size to *N* half-points—not points, half-points! So `\fs24` means 12-point type, `\fs25` means 12½ point type, and `\fs12` means 6-point type. To change the font in the text, use the command `\fN`, where *N* is the number that the document's font table associates with the font we want. For example, here's a document in 12½ point Times (because a `\deff0` says to use the zeroeth font as the default, and a `\fs25` sets the font size for the rest of the document, since it's not in any containing `{...}` group). Except that there's one word, grep, that's in Courier, and one word, "favorite", that's in 15-point type (Example 1).

Example 1. Changing fonts

```
{\rtf1\ansi\deff0 {\fonttbl {\f0 Times;}{\f1 Courier;}}
\fs25
{\pard
You know, {\f1 grep} is my {\fs60 favorite} Unix command!
\par}
}
```

It comes out looking like Figure 9.

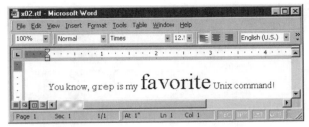

Figure 9. Changing fonts

The reason that the integer argument to \fs is given in half-points instead of full points is to provide a way to express half-points, such as 7½ points. \fs7.5 is bad RTF syntax, as we saw earlier in "Basic RTF Syntax." So measurements are given in half-points, and 7½ can be specified as \fs15.

Advice About {...} Groups

In the code in Example 1, you may wonder about that \fs25 command. Normally it would have a { right before it and would be inside a paragraph, but there it is off on its own! The rule with character formatting commands is that they apply until the end of the currently open {...} group, regardless of whether it was a group that was started right before the command or whether it's been open for some time. The \fs25 command is no exception. Although the \fs25 may seem solitary, there really is an open {...} group: the group that starts with the { that's the first character in this document, and continues until the } that is the last character.

Although I generally advise using character-formatting commands only as a {\command...} construct, this suggestion is to make the resulting RTF easier to debug. It makes no difference to the word processor interpreting the RTF. There are three kinds of cases where it's fine to diverge from this advice:

- When you have character-formatting commands at the start of the document (i.e., after the font table, and before the first paragraph), those formatting commands apply to the whole document. (\fs25 in Example 1 is an example.)

- When you have character-formatting commands at the start of a paragraph, after the \pard, and before any text, those formatting commands apply to the whole paragraph. For example, the \i in {\pard\qc\i...} sets this whole paragraph in italics.

- When you have a series of formatting commands that apply to the same bit of text—i.e., which all turn on at the same time and all turn off at the same time—then you can feel free to turn the by-the-book code {\foo{\bar{\baz...}}} into the more concise {\foo\bar\baz...}. For example, if you wanted "favorite" in 15-point underlined bold italic, you could express that as {\fs30{\ul{\b very favorite}}}, but you could just as well express it as {\fs30\ul\b very favorite}. Either way is absolutely valid RTF.

RTF Escapes

As discussed in "Basic RTF Syntax," there are four kinds of things in RTF syntax: commands (like \foo), groups ({...}), plaintext (like Hello World), and escapes. While there are many commands, there are only four escapes to learn: \'xx, \~, _, and \-.

Escapes

\'xx escapes represent any character in the 0–255 range (0x00–0xFF). In \'xx, xx is the two-character hexadecimal code for the character we want to express. This kind of escape was mentioned in the section "Overview of Simple RTF," in which "ê" was expressed in RTF as \'ea, because "ê" is character 0xEA in Latin-1. The ASCII-RTF character chart in Part IV lists all such escapes, and the section

"Unicode in RTF" discusses the problem of how to represent Unicode characters that are outside the range 0x00-0xFF.

Nonbreaking space

\~ indicates a nonbreaking space. A nonbreaking space is a character that looks like a space. Whereas the word processor can break lines at a space character, it will never do so at a nonbreaking space character. For example, consider the words "Apollo 11", as in the phrase "...crew of Apollo 11 consisted...". If you want the word processor to potentially split "Apollo 11" across lines, you would express it as just:

```
...crew of Apollo 11 consisted...
```

But to keep these words always on the same line, you would instead have:

```
...crew of Apollo\~11 consisted...
```

That way, if the word processor needs to insert a linebreak near "Apollo 11", it will either keep "Apollo 11" together on the current line, or will put it all on the next.

Nonbreaking hyphen

_ indicates a nonbreaking hyphen. A nonbreaking hyphen is a character that looks like a hyphen, but can't be broken across lines as a normal hyphen. For example, if "willy-nilly" is expressed as in this phrase:

```
the EU's willy-nilly expansion
```

It could be laid out with "willy-" at the end of on one line and "nilly" at the start of the next line. To prevent that break, express "willy-nilly" like so:

```
the EU's willy\_nilly expansion
```

My advice is to express every hyphen as a _, except in cases where you know it's safe to break across lines. This avoids confusion in the case of hyphens occurring in email addresses, URLs, and other kinds of computerese. That is, if you were reading a discussion of Lisp functions, and saw the following:

> ...can be achieved with a call to `get-internal-real-time` which returns...

you wouldn't know whether the function is called `get-internal-real-time` or `get-internal-realtime`.

In such cases, either turn hyphenation off for the whole document, or render the word in RTF with nonbreaking hyphens: `get\_internal\_real\_time`. On the other hand, there are cases of odd technical terms in which hyphens don't need to be `\_` characters. These terms can instead be freely line-broken; for example, in chemical names such as "2-chloro-4-ethylamino-6-isopropylamino-1,3,5-triazine".

Hyphenation point

`\-` indicates a hyphenation point. If hyphenation is turned on for the document, the word processor will try to make the text wrap nicely by hyphenating words. But we can't just break a word at any point. For example, "antimatter" can't be broken as "an-timatter," "ant-imatter," or "antima-tter." A word processor knows this by looking up "antimatter" in an internal hyphenation system (for the current language) that lists whole words, prefixes, and generic rules; it so arrives at "anti-matter" or, in a pinch, "antimat-ter." In cases where we have long words that the hyphenation module doesn't know (or just gets wrong), we can use the `\-` escape in order to indicate explicitly where the word can be broken. This step is necessary with words too rare to be known to the word processor's hyphenator, such as "idempotency" (i.e., `idem\-potency`), or long foreign words, such as the German and Sanskrit compounds *Vergangenheitsbewältigung* and *Trimsikavijñaptimatratasiddhih*:

```
Vergangen\-heits\-bew\'e4ltigung
Trimsika\-vij\'f1apti\-matrata\-siddhih
```

Similarly, it's useful to use \- when mentioning long symbol names in Java, like AccessibleAWTCheckboxMenuItem or ChangeToParentDirectoryAction. It's up to the reader what algorithm can best turn AccessibleAWTCheckboxMenuItem into:

```
Accessible\-AWT\-Checkbox\-Menu\-Item
```

The \plain Formatting Command

We close with the most zen of character-formatting commands, \plain. \plain resets the character formatting: it turns off all characteristics—italics, bold, smallcaps, super-script, and so on. Things that can't meaningfully be turned off, like point-size, font number, or language (discussed later in "Incidental Features") are reset to their default values. For example:

```
{\i Or {\b I {\scaps shall {\plain scream!}}}, I shall!}
```

This is rendered as: "*Or **I SHALL** scream!, I shall!*", since the \plain in the innermost group containing the "scream!" resets the characteristics of smallcaps, bold, and italics that this group would otherwise inherit from the containing groups.

In theory, we rarely need the \plain command. However, some word processors have subtle bugs relating to what they think the initial state of character formatting is for a document; these bugs can be avoided by judicious use of the \plain command at the start of a document, explicitly reset-ting all the character formatting. This is discussed in greater detail in the "Document Structure" section.

Incidentally, the exact effect of \plain on font size is prob-lematic. The RTF specification seems to say that \plain should reset the current font size to 12-point, but some versions of MSWord reset it to 10-point. To be sure the point size resets to what you intend, explicitly set it after every \plain, as in "{\scaps shall {\plain\fs24 scream!}}".

Unicode in RTF

Unicode characters are characters over 255, usually in the range 256 to 65,535. For example, the Chinese character 道 is character 36,947, and the character 可 is character 21,487.

Here's how to escape a Unicode character in RTF:

- If the character is 255 or under, use a \'*xy* to express it. For example, the letter "ñ" is character 241. That's 0xF1 in hexadecimal, so it's expressed as \'f1 in RTF. As another example, the mid-dot symbol ("·") is character 183, or 0xB7 in hexadecimal; so it's \'b7 in RTF.

- If the character is between 255 and 32,768, express it as \uc1\u*number**. For example, 可, character number 21,487, is \uc1\u21487* in RTF.

- If the character is between 32,768 and 65,535, subtract 65,536 from it, and use the resulting negative number. For example, 道 is character 36,947, so we subtract 65,536 to get −28,589 and we have \uc1\u-28589* in RTF.

- If the character is over 65,535, then we can't express it in RTF, at least not according to specifications available at the time of this writing. For example, the 𝄞 symbol is character 119,073. We can't express it in RTF. About the best we can do in such cases is to try to find a font that has that character at some lower character number. This method is not as tidy and portable as using a Unicode character, but it's better than nothing. (Or, in complete desperation, you could embed an image of the character; see the section "Embedding Images.")

For example, the first five characters of the *Tao Te Ching* are these:

道·可道·

The ASCII/Unicode character numbers for the characters are:

36,947 183 21,487 36,947 183

Here's how to express it in RTF:

```
\uc1\u-28589*\'b7\uc1\u21487*\uc1\u-28589*\'b7
```

While the above rules hold for normal printable characters, there are four exceptions worth noting: the ASCII newline character, the ASCII form-feed character, the Latin-1 non-breaking space, and the Latin-1 soft hyphen. While we could, in theory, escape these as \'0a, \'0c, \'a0 and \'ad respectively, those escapes are not well supported. It is preferable to use the command \line for newline, the command \page for form-feed, the escape \~ for the nonbreaking space, and the escape \- for the soft hyphen.

Support for the Unicode escapes

Although the specification for expressing Unicode in RTF is over five years old, support for RTF in different applications is still somewhat hit-or-miss.

For example, since no single font is ever likely to be able to render every Unicode character, it is reasonable to expect an application to try to find a font that has a particular Unicode character, if the font you're currently using doesn't have that character. If the current font were Times New Roman, and you want to use one of the above Chinese characters (which Times New Roman presumably doesn't provide), an application would presumably scan the locally installed fonts, find that MS Gothic provides that character, and use that font for that character. The result looks like Figure 10.

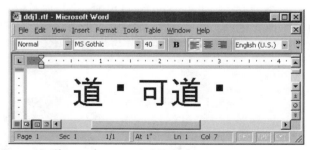

Figure 10. Chinese characters in MS Gothic

MSWord 2000 tries to do that kind of helpful substitution, but it does not do it reliably. Oddly, WordPad (*write.exe*) in MSWin 98 is smarter at this. In any case, in order to use a Unicode character, try to use a font that provides the character. Otherwise, you run the risk of the document coming out looking like Figure 11.

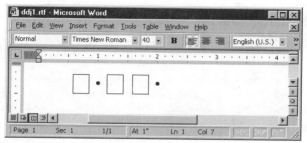

Figure 11. When characters can't be found

Finally, consider the case of RTF readers that don't support Unicode at all. When they see the \uc1\u*number** construct, they parse it as two unknown commands (and therefore ignore them), followed by a "*". Ideally, pre-Unicode RTF readers will parse the *Tao Te Ching* RTF as simply "*.**.".

There are exceptions, however. WordPerfect 8 inexplicably parses the above as " * * *". But this is because WordPerfect 8's RTF support is ghastly in general; it's not specific to just its support for Unicode characters.

Document Structure

So far we've taken an informal approach to the question of how a document is built, basically saying little more than to start the document with a line like this:

```
{\rtf1\ansi\deff0 {\fonttbl {\f0 Times;}{\f1 Courier;}}
```

and then put a } at the very end of the document.

In this section, we'll take a closer look at what can go in a document.

An RTF document consists of a *prolog*, a *font table*, an optional *color table*, an optional *stylesheet*, an optional *info group*, *preliminaries*, content (i.e., all the paragraphs of actually visible text), and then a } at the end.

Document Prolog

An RTF document must start out with these six characters:

```
{\rtf1
```

The 1 indicates the version of RTF being used. Currently, 1 is the only version there has ever been. Given how backward-compatible RTF is, it's doubtful that there will ever be a need for a 2.

After the {\rtf1, the document should declare what character set it uses, if it uses characters (via \'*xx* escapes) in the 0x80-0xFF range. The way to declare a character set is with one of these commands:

\ansi
> The document is in the ANSI character set, also known as Code Page 1252, the usual MSWindows character set. This is basically Latin-1 (ISO-8859-1) with some characters added between 128 and 160. In theory, this is the default for RTF.

\mac
> The document is in the MacAscii character set, the usual character set under old (pre-10) versions of Mac OS.

\pc
> The document is in DOS Code Page 437, the default character set for MS-DOS. Typists with good muscle-memory will note that this is the character set that is still used for interpreting "Alt numeric" codes—i.e., when you hold down Alt and type "130" on the numeric

keypad, it produces a é, because character 130 in CP437 is an é. That is about the only use that CP437 sees these days.

`\pca`

The document is in DOS Code Page 850, also known as the MS-DOS Multilingual Code Page.

For no really good reason, support for these RTF character sets is perfect in some word processors, almost perfect in others (for example, the rare `\pca` command isn't implemented), and shoddy in others (as when only `\ansi` is supported). In a few bad old word processors, these commands are completely ignored, and the document is interpreted as being in whatever character set happens to strike that word processor's fancy. If your document is all characters in the range 0x00–0x7F, then you won't have any problem. The bad news is that you may be using codes outside that range without noticing it, such as smart quotes, long dashes, or the like.

The best advice I can give is to use only the ANSI character set (as it is the best-supported character set) and signal you are using it by starting the document with the `{\rtf1\ansi` code. The `\ansi` can be considered optional, but some applications demand it (as with at least some versions of the Windows Help Compiler, discussed in Part II), and some applications misread its absence as meaning "This document is in the native character set."

After the character set declaration comes the `\deffN` command, which declares that font number *N* is the default font for this document. (What font the number *N* actually indicates is defined in the font table that follows.) Rather like `\ansi`, `\deffN` is technically optional, but you should always put it there. For example, this is a very common prolog, which declares the RTF document to be in the ANSI character set, and picks font 0 as the default font:

```
{\rtf1\ansi\deff0
```

Font Table

A *font table* lists all the fonts that can be used in this document and associates a number with each one. The font table is required, although some programs will tolerate a file that has no font table.

The syntax for a font table is {\fonttbl ...*declarations*...}, in which each declaration has this basic syntax:

```
{\fnumber\familycommand Fontname;}
```

Replace *number* with any integer, and replace *familycommand* with one of the following commands.

Command	Description	Examples
\fmodern	Monospace fonts	Courier New Lucida Console
\froman	Proportionally spaced serif fonts	Arial Times New Roman Bookman Georgia
\fswiss	Proportionally spaced sans serif fonts	Tahoma Lucida Sans Verdana
\fnil	Unknown/Other	

Here is a font table with four declarations:

```
{\fonttbl
{\f0\froman Times;}
{\f1\fswiss Arial;}
{\f2\fmodern Courier New;}
}
```

In a document with that font table, {\f2 stuff} would print "stuff" in Courier New.

You can't use a font in a document unless you declare it in the font table. But you don't have use every font that you list in the font table.

The original intent of having a font family declared with each font—whether \fmodern, \froman, \fswiss, \fnil, or one of the less useful ones that are in the specification but aren't discussed here—was so that if a word processor were reading a document that declared a font that wasn't on the system, the word processor could substitute one of the same family. But it turned out that this feature was hard to implement well, and many word processors don't implement it at all. In practice, you can simply declare every font as \fnil or even leave off the font-family declaration. The RTF specification suggests that the declaration is syntactically needed, but hardly any word processors actually require it; for sake of brevity, almost all the examples in this book leave out the declaration. So far, the only applications I've found that seem to require a font family declaration are the Microsoft Help Compiler, and an old (1.0.3) version of AbiWord.

It is customary to declare \f0, then \f1, then \f2, and so on in order, going up by one each time. But there are word processors that don't follow that convention and the RTF specification does not actually lay out this convention.

Color Table

The *color table* is where you define all the colors that might be used in this document. Once you've defined a color table, you can use the \cf*N* and \cb*N* to change text foreground/background colors, as shown in the section "Changing Text Color." The color table is optional, so there's no reason to include it unless you are using commands like \cf*N* or \cb*N*.

The syntax for a font table is {\colortbl ...*declarations*...}. Each declaration has this basic syntax:

```
\redR\greenG\blueB;
```

where *R*, *G*, and *B* are integers between 0 and 255, expressing the red, green, and blue components of the color being declared. For example, the color orange consists of red at 100% intensity, green at 50% intensity, and blue at 0% intensity. The

RTF declaration of this is \red255\green128\blue0;, which many readers will recognize as akin to the hexadecimal HTML syntax for the same color, #FF8000.

A special declaration syntax of just the character ";" means "default text color". This convention is used for the first entry in the color table. That is, this entry's color isn't any specific color, but should be the default color of whatever format you're rendering this RTF for.[*]

This example color table declares entry 0 with the default text color, entry 1 as red, entry 2 as blue, entry 3 as white, and entry 4a as black:

```
{\colortbl
;
\red255\green0\blue0;
\red0\green0\blue255;
\red255\green255\blue255;
\red0\green0\blue0;
}
```

In this color table, the word "boy" in oh {\cf2 boy}! appears in blue text. See the "Changing Text Color" section for a further discussion of color commands.

Incidentally, you might wonder what the difference would be between \cf4 and \cf0 with the color table above—i.e., what's the difference between the default color, and black? In hardcopy, there is no difference, because the default color for print is black. But on screen, the default color can be anything. For example, suppose MSWindows is running and the Display Properties: Appearance control panel is set to make the default window style appear as white text on a dark blue background. In that case, if you're viewing an RTF document with text that's in the default color, it will show up as

---

[*] Note a subtle difference between "default" in "default text color" and "default" in other uses in this book, as with \deffN. A color table entry of ";" defines the entry in terms of an existing idea of "default text color." But \deffN goes the other way: it defines the idea of "default font" in terms of an existing font table entry. It's a question of defining the default, or using the default to define something else.

white on blue, just like normal text in any other application. But text with an explicit \cf command for black will display as black text. And given that the background color is dark blue, that black text will be quite hard to read—unless, of course, the RTF document also specifies a different background color (such as yellow), in which case, the text will display more readably, as black on yellow.

Stylesheet

A *stylesheet* is where you declare any styles that you might use in the document. A stylesheet is optional. The semantics and usage of stylesheets is discussed in detail later in the "Styles" section, so we will focus just on the syntax here.

The syntax for the stylesheet is {\stylesheet ...*declarations*...}, in which each declaration is either a paragraph style definition or a character style definition. A paragraph style definition has this syntax:

```
{\sA ...formatting commands... \sbasedonB Style Name;}
```

in which A is the number of the style you're defining and B is the number of the style you're basing it on. (If you're not basing it on any style at all, just leave out the \sbasedon*num* command.) For example:

```
{\s7 \qc\li360\sa60\f4\fs20 \sbasedon3 Subsection Title;}
```

This declares a style 7, based on style 3, which has the formatting \qc\li360\sa60\f4\fs20, and is named "Subsection Title". The formatting for paragraph styles can freely mix commands for paragraph formatting (like \qc\li360\sa60) and commands for character formatting (like \f4\fs20). Avoid using commas or semicolons in the style name.

A character style definition has this syntax:

```
{\*\csA \additive ...formatting commands... \sbasedonB Style Name;}
```

in which A is the number of the style you're defining the character style as, and B is the number of the character style you're basing it on. (As before, the \sbasedon*num* command is optional.) The formatting commands here should be just character-formatting commands, without any paragraph-formatting commands. The \additive command is technically optional, but omitting it is not usually what you want. See the "Styles" section for more details.

Here's an example of a character style definition:

```
{\*\cs24 \additive \super\f3 \sbasedon10 IsotopeNum;}
```

This declares a style 24, which has the formatting \super\f3, is based on style 10, and has the name "IsotopeNum".

Incidentally, in both paragraph style and character style definitions, the formatting commands section is free to consist of nothing at all. For example:

```
{\*\cs5 \additive \sbasedon3 AuthorName;}
{\s6 \sbasedon15 Minor Annotation;}
```

The first line declares a *character* style 5, to look just like character style 3, but with the name "AuthorName". The second line declares a *paragraph* style 6, based on style 15 and looking just like it, but with the name "Minor Annotation". Those two styles could be part of a complete stylesheet that looks like this:

```
{\stylesheet
{\*\cs3 Default Paragraph Font;}
{\*\cs5 \additive \sbasedon3 AuthorName;}
{\s6 \sbasedon15 Minor Annotation;}
{\s15 Normal;}
}
```

The RTF specification is not explicit about whether a character style with the same number as a paragraph style is allowed; it's safer to assume it isn't.

Info Group

The optional *info group* stores document metadata. *Metadata* is information that describes the document, but is not actually *in* the document (such as would appear when paging through the document on screen or in hardcopy). The syntax of the info group is {\info ...*metadatafield*...},

where each metadata field has the syntax {*fieldname Value*}.
The RTF specification defines about two dozen metadata
field-name commands (as well as a syntax for declaring addi-
tional field-names), but here we discuss only the following
common fields:

{\title *some title text*}

Declares the document's title. (Note that no formatting
commands are allowed in info group values.) For example, {\title Export Manifest} declares that the document is called "Export Manifest".

{\author *The author's name*}

Declares the author's name. For example, this: {\author
Ren\'e9e Smith} declares "Renée Smith" as the document's author's name.

{\company *The author's affiliation*}

Declares the author's organizational affiliation (corpo-
rate or otherwise). For example, {\company University of
Antarctica}.

{\creatim\yr*Y*\mo*M*\dy*D*\hr*H*\min*M*}

Declares when this document was first created (as
opposed to merely modified). Note that the parameter
for \yr is the real year A.D., \mo is the month number
(January is \mo1), and \hr is the number of the hour in
24-clock (\hr0 is midnight). For example, in the unlikely
event that a document was created at the moment that
the first person set foot on the moon, at July 20, 1969, at
10:56 p.m., it would be expressed as:

{\creatim\yr1969\mo7\dy20\hr22\min56}.

Some programmers may expect \mo1 to mean February,
or might want to express 2001 as \yr101, or might
assume that the time is always in GMT timezone; however, none of those things are correct. Specifically, the
\creatim time is interpreted as the "local" timezone,
although there is no way to declare exactly what

timezone that is. In order to preserve this information, I suggest using \doccomm text.

{\doccomm *Miscellaneous comment text*}

Stores any miscellaneous comments about the document. Useful information to store includes things like the name and version number of the program that produced (or translated) the document (possibly the versions of libraries used), what options were used in generating that document (including what files were the source of the document data), and some expression of the creation time that includes the timezone. For example, one RTF-writing application produces a \doccomm like this:

```
{\doccomm
Pod::Simple::RTF 1.01 using Pod::Simple::PullParser v1.02
under Perl v5.008 at Sat Jan 25 20:44:35 2003 GMT}
}
```

Here's an example information group in an otherwise rather minimal document:

```
{\rtf{\fonttbl{\f0 Georgia;}}
{\info
{\title Reminder to vote tomorrow}
{\author Carrie Chapman Catt}
{\company League of Women Voters}
{\creatim\yr2004\mo11\dy1\hr8\min34}
{\doccomm We're at http://www.lwv.org/}
}
\f0\fs90 Tomorrow is Election Day!
\line Get out and vote!}
```

When this document opens in a word processor, normally all that's visible is the text "Tomorrow is Election Day! Get out and vote!", and that's all that appears when the document is printed. However, most word processors provide some way of viewing (and probably editing) the metadata. In MSWord, it's the File → Properties option, which brings up a multi-tabbed window group. The Summary tab window is shown in Figure 12.

The only metadata field that doesn't appear in Figure 12 is the \creatim value, which appears under the Statistics tab as "Created: November 01, 2004 8:34:00 AM".

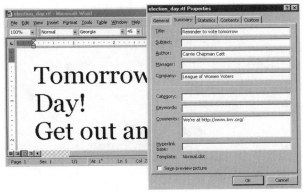

Figure 12. Summary tab window

Defaults for some metadata fields

The \title, \author, \company and \creatim field values get special treatment in MSWord, in this way: if you load a document that doesn't have a value for a field above, MSWord automatically inserts data for those fields. That is, if there's no \author set, MSWord fills in the current user's name. Similarly, if there's no \company set, MSWord fills in the current user's affiliation. (Recall that name and affiliation are generally entered when MSWord is first installed.) If there's no \creatim set, MSWord inserts the current time. And if there's no \title set, MSWord tries to infer it from the text at the start of the document.

This "helpful" feature of MSWord could lead to documents being resaved with an inaccurate mix of the author's and current user's information. To prevent this, always include an info group consisting of at least some values for those keywords, even if the values are just "(see document)" or "X" or some other null-like value. Here's an example that just uses "." as the author name, affiliation, and document title:

```
{\info {\author .}{\company .}{\title .}}
```

If some user opens this document and resaves it, the saved version won't have the user's information dropped into the metadata. MSWord won't put new data into those fields, since the values are already set—even though we as users would hopefully consider those values to be as good as blank.

Preliminaries

Just before the document content starts, you will typically want some formatting commands that affect the document as a whole but that aren't really part of the document. This section can be left empty, but here is a commonly useful string to provide:

```
\deflang1033 \plain \fs26 \widowctrl \hyphauto \ftnbj
{\header \pard\qr\plain\f0\fs16 \chpgn \par}
```

The commands are explained below.

\deflang*number* sets the document's default language to whatever human language that number refers to. The number 1033 is U.S. English, and other language codes are listed in the "RTF Language Codes" section in Part IV. Moreover, language numbers are discussed in greater detail in the "Language Tagging" section. Technically, \deflang chooses a language and declares it when the RTF-reader sees a \plain; later on, the language to reset to is what you're declaring with \deflang.

However, some programs implement \deflang by also making it the initial language value—i.e., the language that text is considered to be in, before any \plain or \lang*Number* sets the language explicitly. You can avoid this whole problem by having a \plain in your Preliminaries section.

A \plain command resets the current font number to whatever was specified in the \deff command. It also resets the font size to 12 points. It resets the language to whatever was specified in the \deflang command. And finally, it turns off all character-formatting features such as underlining, italic, superscript, et cetera. While you can use a \plain command anywhere in a document (just like any other character-formatting command), \plain is most useful here, to make sure that the character-formatting options are explicitly reset at the beginning. In theory, a \plain here isn't necessary, but in practice, having the \plain defeats some bugs in various RTF programs. Moreover, having a \fsN right after a \plain defeats yet more bugs (specifically, some versions of MSWord reset the font size to 10 points instead of 12 points when they see a \plain command).

Next, we have a \fs26 for setting the text size to 13 points. If we want the whole document to be in bold italic, the simplest way would be to just put a \b\i here.

\widowctrl turns on widow and orphan control for this document. This feature is explained in the discussion of the \widctlpar and \nowidctlpar commands (in the section "Paragraphs and Pagebreaks"). Similarly, \hyphauto turns on automatic hyphenation for this whole document. As mentioned in the "Paragraphs" section, automatic hyphenation can be overridden on a per-paragraph basis with \hyphpar0. And \ftnbj means that if you happen to use footnotes in this document, you mean them to be real footnotes instead of endnotes (which is the default).

Finally, the last line is a construct for turning on page numbering in the form of a flush-right 13-point number, in whatever is font number 0 in the font table. You're free to surround the page number (inserted by the \chpgn command) with whatever formatting you like. For example, you could use code like this, which sets the header to "[Doc Title Here / p.1]" (or whatever the page number is) centered at the top, in 11-point italic in font #2, with the "p.1" part in bold:

```
{\header \pard\qc\plain\f2\fs22\i
[ Doc Title Here / {\b p.\chpgn} ]
\par}
```

Content

Content is where all the text considered the "real" document is located. This section is optional, in the sense that you could have a document with no content (such as a document template).

End of Document

Every RTF document must end with a }, to close the group opened by the { that is the first character in the document. Nothing can follow the final }, except possibly a newline.

Incidental Features

This section covers all sorts of odds and ends about RTF. Some of this section discusses features that might not interest you at the moment, but there's something in it for everyone.

The {*\command ... } Construct

From the very beginning, the RTF specification has insisted that if a program sees an RTF command that it doesn't know, it must ignore it and keep going. Consider this text, containing the fictitious commands \zim and \gir:

```
common fallacy that {\b\zim\i scalarity} must \gir774 necessarily
```

A program that doesn't know the commands would read this as if it were:

```
common fallacy that {\b\i scalarity} must necessarily
```

Therefore, developers can use new commands (whether new in the standard, or just for private use) with the certainty that existing RTF programs will react by predictably ignoring the unknown commands—instead of crashing, complaining to the user, or interpreting the command as literal text.

There is a special case of this: the {*\command ...} construct. This special construct means that if the program understands the \command, it takes this to mean {\command ...}, but if it doesn't understand \command, the program ignores not just \command (as it would anyway) but everything in this group. Consider this text, with a fictitious command \bibcit:

```
rather nondualist{\*\bibcit Stcherbatsky 1932{\i b}, p73} and
```

An RTF program that understood the \bibcit command would parse that code as if there were no *. But an RTF program that has never heard of a \bibcit command would treat it as if the whole group weren't there:

```
rather nondualist and
```

Note that all commands and all nested groups are ignored, such as the {\i...} group.

Faking comments with {*\command ... }

RTF is unusual among computer languages in that it doesn't have a syntax for expressing source code comments. That is, in C you can have /* some text */, and in XML and HTML you can use <!-- some text --> but there is no corresponding structure in RTF. {*\command ... } can serve as a comment; all you have to do is use a command that you can be reasonably sure no one will ever implement in any program. For example:

```
{\*\supermegacomment
  Converted from text node 463 in stuff.dat
}
```

That whole group will be ignored by any program that doesn't understand the \supermegacomment command; presumably, that's all programs everywhere, since I just now made up that command name. Regrettably, the command name \comment is taken—as a command for use in the \info section—and so can't just be used anywhere. If it weren't already taken, we could use {*\comment...}.

The only caveat in using a {*\supermegacomment ...} construct (for whatever novel pseudocommand you choose: {*\uvula ...} or {*\octopuselbows ...} work just as well) is that the content has to be syntactically valid RTF. A safe rule of thumb is to avoid any content with a backslash, { or }, or any eight-bit characters.

Language Tagging

A word processor can't spellcheck or hyphenate a stretch of text unless it knows what human language that text is in. The way to express "This text is in language X" is with the \lang*Langnum* command. This command is used like a font formatting command (such as \b or \fs*Halfpoints*), but happens to have no normally visible effect. For example:

```
The SETI projects hope that meaningful communication
with aliens is possible, in spite of Wittgenstein's
supposition that {\lang1031 wenn ein L\'f6we sprechen
k\'f6nnte, wir k\'f6nnten ihn nicht verstehen}.
```

In that sentence, the appearance of the phrase "Wenn ein Löwe sprechen könnte, wir könnten ihn nicht verstehen" is no different than the surrounding text when shown on the screen or printed on the page. The \lang1031 command says that this text is in German (1031 indicates German, as listed in the "RTF Language Codes" section in Part IV), whereas the larger document is presumably tagged as some form of English (such as 1033 for U.S. English). This language would be expressed with a \lang1033 earlier on, or expressed with a \deflang1033\plain at the start of the document, as discussed earlier in the "Preliminaries" section.

But what does this language-tagging actually do? At the very least, having tagged that phrase as German tells the word processor that it's not English, and the English spellchecker shouldn't scan it. With an occasional foreign word in a short document, this distinction usually isn't worth the bother, but if your document is long and full of foreign words or quotes, spellchecking it can be tedious without language tagging; the word processor would constantly catch apparently misspelled words like "wenn", "ein", "Löwe", and so on. Even if you don't mean for a document to be deliberately spellchecked, bear in mind that most word processors now automatically check every document they open, and put wavy red lines under unknown words. To keep those distractions away from foreign words, use language tagging.

But language tagging doesn't just indicate whether text is to be spellchecked. If the user's word processor installation happens to have a German spellcheck module, then the word processor should actually use that for spellchecking text in \lang1031 (German)—so that if "sprechen" were mistyped as "psrechen", the word processor would know to mark it as wrong and suggest "sprechen".

Moreover, if the document is hyphenated, tagging text as German means that English hyphenation rules don't apply, and a German hyphenation module should be used, if available.

Text that's not really in any human language at all, such as computer code, can be tagged as \lang1024. This indicates that the text is in a "null" language. For example:

```
and inside was a mysterious coded message
reading "{\lang1024 JRNRL LDKCM UXFGM}".  She
```

or:

```
by using the {\lang1024 tcgetpgrp} function for
```

RTF has a new command, \noproof, which labels text as immune to spellchecking but otherwise still in the same language as the surrounding text. For example:

```
making what Chaucer would call a {\noproof "pilgrymage
to Caunterbury with ful devout corage"}, in spite of
```

However, since this is a new command, older programs that don't know it ignore it, and blithely treat the text inside as still spellcheckable. If this isn't a problem, you can just use a plain \noproof as above. But for backwards-compatibility, use the circumlocution \lang1024\noproof\langnp*Langnum*, in which *Langnum* repeats the language code of the surrounding text. This new \langnp command means the same thing as \lang, but was introduced at the same time as \noproof.

Consider how this text would be interpreted by an old program and a new program:

```
call a {\lang1024\noproof\langnp1033 "pilgrymage..."}, in
```

An old RTF program sees and understands the \lang1024, and knows the following text is in the null language; the old program sees \noproof and \langnp1033, but it is ignorant of each code, and ignores them both. An old program treats "pilgrymage..." as part of the null language. A new RTF program would see and understand \lang1024 as before, then see \noproof and turn off spellchecking, and see \langnp1033, which resets the current language back to 1033. A new program treats "pilgrymage..." as part of whatever language \langnp (re)declares—in this case, 1033 for U.S. English, the language of the surrounding text.

The \lang1024\noproof\langnp*Langnum* idiom is roundabout, but effective.

The difference between these two bits of text:

```
{\lang1024 "pilgrymage to Caunterbury with ful devout corage"}
```

```
{\lang1024\noproof\langnp1033 "pilgrymage to Caunterbury with
ful devout corage"}
```

is that the second one is subject to English hyphenation rules, whereas the second one isn't, since it's in the null language.

Other, rarer word-processor features might use language tagging. For example, if a user applies a thesaurus function to the word "devout" in the second bit of code (in MSWord, this is just a matter of right-clicking on the word and selecting "Synonyms" on the menu that pops up), the word processor knows to use the English synonym dictionary. But if the user tries this in the first bit of code, the word processor will presumably give an error, since it won't have any synonym dictionary for the null language. Some formatting behavior can be language-dependent: the "ck" character pair often kerns more closely in German; the smallcaps command, \scaps, operates slightly differently in Turkish; line-justification may have to use a different algorithm for Thai;

and so on. Language tagging may also be needed if you are sending text to a speech synthesizer or to a Braille printer.

Newspaper Columns

Columns used in context of text usually bring to mind tables; they're covered in the "Tables" section of Part I. RTF also supports a quite different feature with a similar name: newspaper columns.

Normally, a word processor lays out a page's content in one pass from top to bottom. When the word processor instead breaks the content into several columns, filling the first before adding text to the second, the format is *newspaper columns*. A layout with newspaper columns is can make pages with small print or frequent linebreaks much easier to read. While the term "newspaper columns" obviously brings to mind newspapers, examples of this kind of layout are often to be found in dictionaries and indexes.

The way to switch layout to newspaper column mode is to use the \cols*N* command, in which *N* is the number of columns per page. Typically you will use only \cols2, \cols3, or \cols4; more than four columns per page is generally hard to read.

By default, there is no line between the columns. To draw a line between them, add a \linebetcol command.

By default, the columns are separated by a distance of 720 twips—i.e., a half inch, or about 12mm. To set this gap to a different value, use the \colsx*Twips* command, in which *Twips* is the distance in twips. For example, to make the columns a full inch apart, use \colsx1440. To reduce it to a quarter-inch, use \colsx360.

This bit of code lays out text in three columns, sets the distance between the columns at 567 twips (10mm), and draws a line between them (there's 5mm on each side of the line):

```
\cols3
\colsx567
\linebetcol
...paragraphs...
```

The last page of text laid out that way will look something like Figure 13.

Figure 13. Newspaper column layout

Columns and sections

A \colsN command might be expected to take effect right where it occurs in the text, not before or after. But this is not actually the case: wherever the command occurs, it affects the whole section. A section is a concept we haven't yet discussed; it is a logical division of the document. Just as a paragraph-formatting command like \li sets the left indent value for an entire paragraph, a \cols command sets the number of columns for an entire section. (Putting these commands at the start of the paragraph/section is a syntactic requirement in some cases, but in other cases, it just makes the code more human-readable. In either case, it's a good idea.)

Sections are not discussed elsewhere in this book, because they only come up in certain formatting features that are beyond the scope of this condensed guide. The only notable exceptions are page header settings and newspaper columns. Follow these rules of thumb in order to avoid bothering with sections:

- If you want a whole document in columns, put a \cols*N* command at the start of the document, right after the document preliminaries. Follow the \cols*N* with the optional \colsx*Distance* and \linebetcol commands.

- If you want to have a document partly in columns, switch to column modes with \sectd\sect and the \cols*N* command. You can change out of column mode later with \sectd\sect code.

  Whenever you use a \sectd\sect, it has the side effect of turning off the page-numbering header mentioned earlier in the "Preliminaries" section. So if you used that code, you have to repeat it after \sectd\sect. The document would look like this:

```
document starts...
{\header \pard\qr\plain\f0\fs16 \chpgn \par}
...some paragraphs not in columns, and then...
\sectd\sect
{\header \pard\qr\plain\f0\fs16 \chpgn \par}
\cols3 \colsx567 \linebetcol
...some paragraphs that get put in columns...
\sectd\sect
{\header \pard\qr\plain\f0\fs16 \chpgn \par}
...some paragraphs not in columns...
...document ends
}
```

For more details on the notion of sections, look under the heading "Section Formatting Properties" in the RTF specification.

Footnotes

Insert footnotes in RTF text using this construct:

```
{\super\chftn}{\footnote\pard\plain\chftn ...text here...}
```

The \footnote construct is actually used for inserting notes of various kinds—proper footnotes, or endnotes with various

---

formatting quirks. The default is to create endnotes. This default might be a surprise, considering the command name is \footnote and not \endnote. To make \footnote commands actually produce footnotes, put a \ftnbj command in the Preliminaries part of a document (as discussed earlier in the "Preliminaries" section of this book). The name \ftnbj stands for "footnote bottom-justified". The default footnote numbering behavior is "1, 2, 3, ..." (as opposed to "i, ii, iii, ...", for example) and for numbering to not reset at the end of the page.

For a full discussion of footnote numbering styles and the complexities of endnote placement, refer to the RTF specification. A \ftnbj at the start of the document and the footnote construct shown here should behave as is expected for normal English text. For example:

```
so called "minority languages", as in North America
{\super\chftn}{\footnote\pard\plain\chftn
: See {\i Navajo Made Easier} by Irvy Goosen}
, Europe
{\super\chftn}{\footnote\pard\plain\chftn
: See {\i Who's Afraid of Luxembourgish?} by Jul Christophory}
 and the Mediterranean
{\super\chftn}{\footnote\pard\plain\chftn
: See {\i Learn Maltese, Why Not?} by Joseph Vella}
, to name but a few.
```

When formatted as part of a larger document, this code looks like Figure 14.

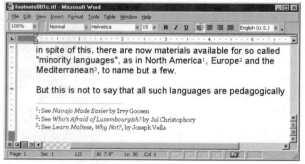

Figure 14. Footnote formatting

The RTF specification doesn't stipulate how or whether foot-notes should inherit font, character, or paragraph formatting from the paragraph they're anchored to. The safest approach is to include a \pard\plain to reset to document defaults (as shown above), and then add any commands you want in order to select a different font, point size, et cetera.

Changing Text Color

The "Color Table" section in "Document Structure" dis-cussed the syntax for declaring color tables. Here's where we actually use them, to set the foreground and background color of text.

First, assume that a document has this color table right after its font table:

```
{\colortbl
;
\red255\green0\blue0;
\red0\green0\blue255;
}
```

As explained earlier, this declares a palette with three entries:

Palette entry 0: the default color
Palette entry 1: red (#FF0000)
Palette entry 2: blue (#0000FF)

The \cf*ColorNum* command is a character-formatting com-mand that sets the text color to whatever palette entry num-ber *ColorNum* was defined to be. So, given the above color table, {\cf1 yow!} puts the word "yow!" in red type.

The RTF specification also defines a command (\cb*ColorNum*) that does for the background of the text what \cf*ColorNum* does for the foreground. For example, if you had {\cb5 yow!} and defined palette entry 5 as light yellow, it would look like the word "yow!" had been gone over with a highlighter pen. But in one of the few cases I've yet found of Microsoft com-pletely disregarding their own RTF specification, MSWord simply does not implement the \cb command. Instead, it implements exactly the same function with a different construct: \chshdng0\chcbpat*ColorNum*, in which *ColorNum* is the same number as would be used in a \cb*ColorNum* command.

Regrettably, MSWord seems to be the only word processor at present that understands the \chshdng0\chcbpat*ColorNum* construct; so in order to set the background color, you should use \chshdng0\chcbpat*ColorNum* and \cb*ColorNum*:

```
{\chshdng0\chcbpat5\cb5 yow!}
```

Moreover, to set the text foreground *or* background color, it's best to set both of them, to ensure that they display correctly on screen. For example:

```
{\cf4\chshdng0\chcbpat5\cb5 yow!}
```

See the end of the "Color Table" section for a discussion of the rationale for this.

Hyperlinks

The construct for making text into a hyperlink to a specific URL is rather large:

```
There are examples and errata at
{\field{\*\fldinst{HYPERLINK
 "http://www.oreilly.com/catalog/rtfpg/"
}}{\fldrslt{\ul
this book's web site
}}}.
```

This expresses the sentence "There are examples and errata at this book's web site." The phrase "this book's web site" is underlined and serves as a hyperlink to the URL *http://www.oreilly.com/catalog/rtfpg/*. If you also want to make it blue, add a color-change command, as from the above section, like this:

```
There are examples and errata at
{\field{\*\fldinst{HYPERLINK
 "http://www.oreilly.com/catalog/rtfpg/"
}}{\fldrslt{\ul\cf2
this book's web site
}}}.
```

That, of course, assumes there's a color table that declares a color #2.

Page Margins

In the section "Paragraph Indenting," we discussed the \li and \ri commands for controlling the indenting of paragraphs. Indenting (in this sense) means the distance from the left or right margin of the page. But the margins aren't carved in stone—they can be redefined at will.

To control the placement of the margins, use the following commands in a document. They should go in the Preliminaries section, presumably before page numbering is turned on:

\margtN
> Top margin, in twips (the default is 1440).

\margbN
> Bottom margin, in twips (the default is 1440).

\marglN
> Left margin, in twips (the default is 1800).

\margrN
> Right margin, in twips (the default is 1800).

For example, in order to provide a larger-than-normal left margin, use \margl2880 to indicate that the left margin is 2,880 twips (2 inches) from the left edge of the actual page.

Page Size and Orientation

Few RTF documents need to stipulate the size of the page that they were formatted for. A word processor generally has a notion of whether it typically prints to "U.S. letter" paper (8.5" x 11") or to the narrower and taller A4 paper (210mm x 297mm) used outside the U.S. If a document doesn't force one size of paper or another, the word processor will format the document with the default paper-size.

If you're printing normal documents (i.e., portrait-orientation formatting on the default paper size for your default printer), you won't need any special RTF commands. But to print in landscape mode (i.e., sideways), or to otherwise change page orientation or size, you must to consider the size of paper.

To print a document in landscape mode on U.S. letter paper, put this code in the document's Preliminaries section, presumably before turning on page numbering:

```
\paperw15840 \paperh12240
\margl1440 \margr1440 \margt1800 \margb1800
\landscape
```

If you want landscape mode for A4-sized paper, use this instead:

```
\paperw16834 \paperh11909
\margl1440 \margr1900 \margt1800 \margb1800
\landscape
```

If you want to print in *two-up* format (i.e., two virtual pages sideways on one physical page, a.k.a. *journal preprint style*), use this code for U.S. letter paper:

```
\paperw7920 \paperh12240
\margl1440 \margr1440 \margt1800 \margb1800
\twoonone\landscape
```

This is the code for getting the same effect for A4 paper:

```
\paperw8417 \paperh11909
\margl1440 \margr1843 \margt1800 \margb1800
\twoonone\landscape
```

Note that in each case, the margin settings (the middle line in each) are simply an initial recommendation; you may actually want larger or smaller margins. And when printing in two-up format, you will almost definitely want to use a smaller font size than the default 12-point.

Line Drawing

RTF has a happily large but regrettably convoluted system for representing graphics primitives such as lines, arcs, circles, polygons, and so on. The simple task of representing a 5-inch horizontal rule requires this much code:

```
{\pard {\*\do
\dobxcolumn \dobypara \dodhgt7200
```

```
\dpline \dpptx0 \dppty0 \dpptx7200
\dppty0 \dpx0 \dpy0 \dpxsize7200
\dpysize0 \dplinew15
\dplinecor0 \dplinecog0 \dplinecob0 }\par}
```

That line can be made longer or shorter by replacing the three instances of 7200 with some other length in twips.

If you want more complex graphics in RTF, the simplest method is probably to just embed a real image, as covered in the next section. But if you want to learn more about RTF's graphics primitives, see the section "Drawing Objects" in the RTF specification. Also, have a look at the Origami CD Case example in Part III, which involves plotting lines between arbitrary points on the page, using a variant of the code shown above.

Here is another way to draw a horizontal line:

```
{\pard \brdrb \brdrs \brdrw10 \brsp20 \par}
{\pard\par}
```

That code is rather more compact, but also works in a basically different way. Where the previous code inserts a paragraph containing an attached line-drawing primitive, this approach inserts a blank paragraph with a border along its bottom; then a borderless blank paragraph is inserted so that there will be as much space below the line as above it. (This book does not discuss the general case of paragraph borders, but the RTF Specification explains them in its "Paragraph Borders" section.)

A more practical explanation of the difference between these two approaches to line-drawing is that the first requires you to say exactly how long you want the line to be; in the second approach, the line runs from margin to margin, because it is simply the width of the blank paragraph that it's based on.

You can make the border-based line shorter by narrowing its blank paragraph using the normal \li*Twips* and \ri*Twips* commands described in the "Paragraphs" section. For example, this code draws a horizontal line that starts 4cm (2,268 twips) in from the left margin and ends 1cm (567 twips) in from the right margin:

```
{\pard \li2268 \ri567
\brdrb \brdrs \brdrw10 \brsp20 \par}
{\pard\par}
```

The actual length of the resulting line depends on the current settings for the page margin (or, the document is in columns, the current column size).

Whether you use the first or second approach might simply depend on which is best supported in a particular word processor. For example, WordPerfect 8 understands the first line-drawing approach much better. But most other word processors either understand both, or don't understand either.

Embedding Images

In an ideal world, RTF would allow you to insert a picture into a document by simply dropping a hex-encoded GIF, JPEG, or PNG file into your RTF code. But RTF doesn't do things that way. The RTF specification, on the subject of pictures, explains a {\pict...} construct that contains picture data (typically as a long series of hexadecimal digits). But the picture data encoded in the {\pict...} construct is in a binary format that can't be converted to easily from a conventional image format (i.e., GIF, JPEG, or PNG).

If you want to insert images in an RTF file, you have three options. The first option is to give up and do without the image. In many cases, the image isn't necessary (as with a company logo on an invoice document).

The second option is to produce the binary encoding of the image by copying it out of an RTF file generated by a word processor. So if you want to insert a logo in an invoice that you're autogenerating as RTF, you could start AbiWord (for example), start a new blank file, insert a picture from disk, save the file as *.rtf*, and then open the *.rtf* file in a text editor.

For example, inserting a 2 x 2 blue dot in AbiWord produces an RTF file that ends like this:

```
\pard\plain\ltrpar\s15{\*\shppict
{\pict\pngblip\picw2\pich2\picwgoal28\pichgoal28
\bliptag10000{\*\blipuid 00000000000000000000000000002710}
89504e470d0a1a0a0000000d494844520000000200000002040300000000809810
1700000003050c4c544500000008000000080008000000808000800080808080
80c0c0c0ff000000ff00ffff000000ffff00ff00ffffffffff7b1fb1c4000000
0c49444154789c6338c3700600033401997bc924ce0000000049454e44ae4260
82}}{\f4\fs24\lang1033{\*\listtag0}}}
```

This image could be copied into other documents by copying the {\pict...} group and inserting it directly into another document as needed. (Note that it must be copied from {\pict up to the next *matching* }, not just the next }. Otherwise, you end up stopping prematurely, at the end of the third line above.)

The third way to insert images in an RTF file is to use this quite nonstandard code to have the word processor insert an arbitrary external image file into the document:

```
{\field\fldedit{\*\fldinst { INCLUDEPICTURE  \\d
"PicturePath"
\\* MERGEFORMATINET }}{\fldrslt { }}}
```

In the *PicturePath*, path separators must either be a forward slash, like so:

```
{\field\fldedit{\*\fldinst { INCLUDEPICTURE  \\d
"C:/stuff/Group_x/images/alaska_map.gif"
\\* MERGEFORMATINET }}{\fldrslt { }}}
```

or must be a double-backslash, escaped (either as \'5c\'5c or as \\\\), like so:

```
{\field\fldedit{\*\fldinst { INCLUDEPICTURE  \\d
"C:\'5c\'5cstuff\'5c\'5cGroup_x\'5c\'5cimages\'5c\'5calaska_map.
gif"
\\* MERGEFORMATINET }}{\fldrslt { }}}
```

or:

```
{\field\fldedit{\*\fldinst { INCLUDEPICTURE  \\d
"C:\\\\stuff\\\\Group_x\\\\images\\\\alaska_map.gif"
\\* MERGEFORMATINET }}{\fldrslt { }}}
```

At time of this writing, this whole image-via-\field construct seems to be particular to MSWord versions, beginning with Word 2000. Other word processors either just ignore the construct (as AbiWord, Wordpad, and others do), or they throw an error (like MSWord Viewer 97, which replaces the image with the text "Error! Unknown switch argument").

You can control exact positioning of an image on the page by simply making it the content of an exact-positioned paragraph, as discussed at the end of the "Basic RTF Syntax" section. For example, this image's top-left corner starts 2,160 twips across and 3,600 twips down from the page's top-left corner:

```
{\pard \pvpg\phpg \posx2160 \posy3600
\field...} or {\pict...}
\par}
```

Overstrike in RTF

Some word-processing programs, such as WordPerfect, support a feature called *overstrike*, in which two (or more) characters can be printed one on top of each other. For example, an overstrike consisting of B and | would give you ฿ , which happens to be the (otherwise usually unavailable) symbol for the Thai currency, the baht. Unfortunately, there's no way to express overstrikes in RTF, and no workaround that I know of.

Centering Vertically and Horizontally

Title pages are typically centered horizontally and vertically; there is as much space on the right side of a line as on the left, and there is as much space added on top of the page's text as below it. A good way to do this is to place a paragraph in the page's center with \pvmrg\phmrg\posxc\posyc\qc, and then follow the paragraph with a pagebreak. Within the paragraph, you can add \line commands to force linebreaks.

For example, this code can serve as the title page of a document (Figure 15):

```
{\pard \pvmrg\phmrg\posxc\posyc \qc
\fs60 {\i Motherboard, May I?}
\line
```

```
\line\fs50 Screenplay by S. Burke
\line\fs40 Draft 7\par}

{\pard \page \par}
```

Figure 15. A centered page

Often, the text looks better slightly higher on the page than exact centering would put it. To get this effect, put a \line or two before the \par} in the centered paragraph.

This \pvmrg\phmrg\posxc\posyc construct is a variant of the commands discussed earlier in the "Exact Paragraph Positioning" part of the "Paragraphs" section. These commands are explained in greater detail in the "Positioned Objects and Frames" section of the RTF Specification.

Symbols

If you want an unusual symbol in a document while using a language like TeX, insert a command for it—like \infin, to get the infinity symbol. RTF avoids this approach, instead opting for an approach in which you select a font that provides a particular character and then insert that character, often with a \'xx sequence.

For example, the font called simply "Symbol" comes with MSWindows and provides several dozen common technical characters, as well as some line-drawing characters. Figure 16 shows all the characters available in the Symbol font, in rows by the first hex digit of the \'xx sequence and in columns by the second hex digit. For example, to insert an infinity symbol in a document, use \fFontnum to switch to the Symbol font, then follow it with \'a5, as in {\f3\'a5}.

	\'_0	\'_1	\'_2	\'_3	\'_4	\'_5	\'_6	\'_7	\'_8	\'_9	\'_a	\'_b	\'_c	\'_d	\'_e	\'_f
\'2_		!	∀	#	∃	%	&	∋	(	)	∗	+	,	−	.	/
\'3_	0	1	2	3	4	5	6	7	8	9	:	;	<	=	>	?
\'4_	≅	Α	Β	Χ	Δ	Ε	Φ	Γ	Η	Ι	ϑ	Κ	Λ	Μ	Ν	Ο
\'5_	Π	Θ	Ρ	Σ	Τ	Υ	ς	Ω	Ξ	Ψ	Ζ	[	∴	]	⊥	_
\'6_		α	β	χ	δ	ε	φ	γ	η	ι	φ	κ	λ	μ	ν	ο
\'7_	π	θ	ρ	σ	τ	υ	ϖ	ω	ξ	ψ	ζ	{	|	}	~	
\'a_		ϒ	′	≤	⁄	∞	ƒ	♣	♦	♥	♠	↔	←	↑	→	↓
\'b_	°	±	″	≥	×	∝	∂	•	÷	≠	≡	≈	…	|	—	↵
\'c_	ℵ	ℑ	ℜ	℘	⊗	⊕	∅	∩	∪	⊃	⊇	⊄	⊂	⊆	∈	∉
\'d_	∠	∇	®	©	™	∏	√	⋅	¬	∧	∨	⇔	⇐	⇑	⇒	⇓
\'e_	◊	〈	®	©	™	∑	⎛	|	⎝	⎡	|	⎣	⎧	|	⎩	|
\'f_	□	〉	∫	⌠	|	⌡	⎞	|	⎠	⎤	|	⎦	⎫	|	⎭	□

Figure 16. Symbol font

The section "Character Formatting" discusses the Unicode extensions to RTF, which provide a way to access symbols by their Unicode character number.

Styles

The RTF constructs that we've covered so far have had syntaxes that seem to match up well with the feature. For example, we think of footnotes as depending on the point in the text where the little footnote-number goes, and accordingly, that's the where we put the {\footnote...} construct. So far, the only real inconveniences we've encountered have been abstractions like font tables, and the occasional bother of unintuitive commands or arguments (such as having to remember that \fs specifies the size in half-points rather than points).

Things get difficult with styles, because the syntax for styles doesn't quite match how we, as word-processor users, are used to thinking about them. Moreover, styles are useful only in documents that are meant to be edited by users who will want to change what the styles mean. If that doesn't describe your documents and their uses, feel quite free to skip this section.

Styles as the User Experiences Them

Suppose you're typing up a bunch of announcements like this:

> On February 19th, we at Keystone Kable TV will change the channel line-up. CSPAN will move from channel 18 to channel 17. CSPAN-2 will move from channel 19 to channel 18. And a new channel, Classic Arts Showcase, will be on channel 19. All hail cable television!!

Now, suppose you want some formatting on "CSPAN", "CSPAN-2", and "Classic Arts Showcase". If you want bold-face, you could just click on each and make them bold. But you're not sure how you want the words to look. You don't want to have to put them each in one kind of formatting (like 13-point italic Lucida Sans), then decide you don't like it and have to go back to every word and undo the formatting and then put it in some different formatting (like smallcaps Bookman with a "don't spellcheck this" command). Repetitive formatting can be a problem, and that's the problem that styles are meant to solve.

Instead, define a style called "ChannelName", select each of the channel names, and put them in the ChannelName style. Then you can change the definition of the style to whatever you like, try it out, and any changes are automatically reflected in each of the word in the text where the style is used. Changing things in one place (the definition of the ChannelNames style) instead of in several places (each use of a channel name) avoids the repetitive, manual, and potentially error-prone task of changing each instance.

Styles as They Are Represented

The subjective experience of making and editing styles is based on a model that has two parts: first, a declaration of a style: "ChannelName is 13-point italic Bookman"; and then instances of using each style, like "turn on ChannelName, then have CSPAN-2"). You might expect the way to express this in RTF would be something that says "ChannelName is \fs26\i\f1" and then uses it simply, like: "{*now-use-Channel-Name* CSPAN-2}".

But surprisingly, that's not the way RTF does it. RTF styles have two distinct parts; first, a part that means—as expected—"ChannelName is \fs26\i\f1." Then, in the actual use of the style, the code means "{*ChannelName, that is:*\fs26\i\f1 CSPAN-2}". In other words, you have a code that means "now ChannelName!", but you use it *in addition to* the codes that the ChannelName style consists of. This is a basic problem in the design of RTF, and I know of no way around it. Apparently, the regrettable decision was made that having style codes take the place of their constituent codes would require too much complexity in RTF readers.

RTF distinguishes two different kinds of styles: paragraph and character styles. A paragraph style contains commands that control paragraph formatting, namely indenting, justification/centering, spacing before and after the paragraph, and all the other commands discussed in "Basic RTF Syntax." A character style contains commands that control character formatting, such as font choice, point size, bold, italics, and all the other commands discussed in "Character Formatting," in addition to color-change commands and language commands as discussed in the section "Incidental Features."

RTF Stylesheet Syntax

As mentioned in "Document Structure," the way to declare a style is in the *stylesheet* section of the document, right after the font table and the optional color table. Each style is given a number as well as a name, and then actual uses of the style refer to the style number. (This is similar to the way the font table and font uses work.)

The stylesheet consists of {\stylesheet ...*declarations*...} in which each declaration is either a paragraph style definition or a character style definition. A paragraph style definition has this syntax:

```
{\sA ...formatting commands... \sbasedonB Style Name;}
```

A is the number of the style you're defining and B is the number of the style you're basing it on. If you're not basing it on any style, leave out the \sbasedon*num* command. Basing a style on another style means if the user alters the original style, the word processor can update the styles based on it.

A character style definition has this syntax:

```
{\*\csA \additive ...formatting commands... \sbasedonB Style Name;}
```

A is the number you're defining the character style as, and B is the number of the character style you're basing it on. (As before, the \sbasedon*num* command is optional.)

Avoid using commas or semicolons in style names; word processors behave oddly that have styles with commas or semicolons in their declarations.

It is common for a stylesheet to define a paragraph style called "Normal" that is based on no other styles and has few or no paragraph-formatting commands. Similarly, most stylesheets also declare a character style called "Default Paragraph Font" that is based on no other styles and has few or no character-formatting commands. For example:

```
{\fonttbl {\f0\fswiss Arial;}{\f1\froman Bookman;}}

{\stylesheet
{\s0 Normal;}}
```

```
{\*\cs1 Default Paragraph Font;}
...then any other styles...
}
```

To declare a ChannelName style as we were considering earlier, we would add commands like this:

```
{\stylesheet
{\s0 Normal;}
{\*\cs1 Default Paragraph Font;}
{\*\cs2 \additive \fs26\i\f1 \sbasedon1 ChannelName;}
}
```

The ChannelName style (i.e., style #2, a character style) would then be used like this:

```
{\pard
On February 19{\super th}, we at Keystone Kable TV will
  change the channel line-up.
  {\cs2 \fs26\i\f1 CSPAN} will move from channel 18 to channel 17.
  {\cs2 \fs26\i\f1 CSPAN-2} will move from channel 19 to channel 18.
  And a new channel,
  {\cs2 \fs26\i\f1 Classic Arts Showcase}, will
  be on channel 19.  All hail cable television!!
\par}
```

It's simple to declare another style called "PromoChannel-Name" based on the ChannelName style, with the addition of the formatting command for boldface. This new group would go in the stylesheet:

```
{\*\cs3 \additive \fs26\i\f1\b \sbasedon2 PromoChannelName;}
```

It could then be used in the document like this:

```
{\pard
As a bonus, channel 20 will show
  {\cs3 \fs26\i\f1\b HBO-Espa\'f1ol} free for a month!
\par}
```

Making some paragraph formatting into a paragraph style uses a slightly different syntax, but is otherwise the same. In the stylesheet, we would declare a new style like this:

```
{\s4 \li560\sa180 \sbasedon0 Listing_Item;}
```

Then we would use it in the document like this:

```
{\pard \s4 \li560\sa180 17: CSPAN \par}
{\pard \s4 \li560\sa180 18: CSPAN-2 \par}
{\pard \s4 \li560\sa180 19: Classic Arts Showcase \par}
{\pard \s4 \li560\sa180 20: HBO-Espa\'f1ol \par}
```

Note that the spaces on either side of \s4 are optional; they are added for readability. As discussed in "Basic RTF Syntax," a single space at the very end of a command is ignored, and has no effect.

\sbasedon and Style Updating

Note that PromoChannelName declaration has a \sbasedon2 to express that it's based on the ChannelName style. If the user opens the word processor's style editor and changes the definition for ChannelName (for example, to use a different font), the word processor can apply the changes to Promo-ChannelName. (Whether it prompts the user for confirmation, or does this automatically, is just a detail of the word processor's interface.)

In fact, if the user changes the Default Paragraph Font style, it affects the ChannelName style (since its declaration says it's based on Default Paragraph Font), which will in turn affect PromoChannelName.

\additive on character style declarations

So far we have been using the \additive option in character style declarations without explanation. This option means that when you use a particular style, its formatting adds to any formatting already in effect. For example, our ChannelName style means "13-point Bookman italic". Imagine using this style in a larger stretch of text that is in boldface. If Channel-Name is declared as \additive, the text in this use of Channel-Name will be in bold, in addition to being 13-point Bookman italic. But if ChannelName isn't declared as \additive, text with that style will only be in 13-point Bookman italic, ignoring boldface or whatever other character formatting might be in use in the surrounding text.

Generally, \additive is what you want and expect, and I have never come across a problem that was solved by leaving it out.

Generating RTF: With or without styles?

At the beginning of this section, I stated that styles are useful only in documents that are meant to be edited by users who will want to change what the styles mean.

Suppose you are writing a little Perl program that makes a chart of what stations are on what channel numbers, and it involves code like this:

```
foreach $channel (@normal_channels) {
  print RTF '{\pard \li560\sa180 ', $channel, '\par}';
}
print RTF '{\pard \line\line Digital Cable Channels\line\par}';
foreach $channel (@digital_channels) {
  print RTF '{\pard \li560\sa180 D:', $channel, '\par}';
}
```

Now, if you want to abstract out the \li560\sa180, you could do it like this:

```
$channel_item = '\li560\sa180';

foreach $channel (@normal_channels) {
  print RTF '{\pard', $channel_item, ' ', $channel, '\par}';
}
print RTF '{\pard \line\line Digital Cable Channels\line\par}';
foreach $channel (@digital_channels) {
  print RTF '{\pard', $channel_item, ' D:', $channel, '\par}';
}
```

In the program that generates the RTF, you use $channel_item as often as you want, but you define it in only one place—the one place where you'd change the definition if you wanted to change all the uses of $channel_item.

Notice that if this program uses RTF styles, it's no shorter, and no more convenient:

```
$channel_item = '\li560\sa180';

...right after the font table...
print RTF '{\stylesheet
{\s0 Normal;}
...some styles...
{\s4 ', $channel_item, ' \sbasedon0 Listing_Item;}
...some styles...
}
';
```

```
...then later...
foreach $channel (@normal_channels) {
  print RTF '{\pard \s4', $channel_item, ' ', $channel, '\par}';
}
print RTF '{\pard \line\line Digital Cable Channels\line\par}';
foreach $channel (@digital_channels) {
  print RTF '{\pard \s4', $channel_item, ' D:', $channel, '\par}';
}
```

The only difference between this document and the style-less one is that if the user wanted to open the document and change the formatting of every Listing_Item at once, clearly he could do so only with the document that actually defines and uses a Listing_Item style.

If you want your RTF-generating program to have less redundancy, the way to do that is to use variables (or subroutines, or constants) as we did with $channel_item above. Styles won't help you there; they are useful only in interactive editing of documents.

Tables

Tables are always complicated, whether we're talking about the abstract concept of tables in any markup language, or getting a particular table to look just right in a particular document. These warnings are particularly apt in RTF, because tables are just about the only RTF feature that makes MSWord crash if they're not done correctly. You're likely to find your enthusiasm for pretty formatting waning as you watch MSWord crash for the tenth time in a minute, requiring the third reboot in the past hour, possibly after MSWord has corrupted the document beyond repair.

My advice is learn a small, safe subset of table syntax, and use just that. This section covers only a part of the large (and ever-expanding) syntax for tables as covered in the RTF Specification.

One Row at a Time

RTF has no single construct that expresses a table. Instead, RTF has a construct for expressing a row, and a table consists of a series of independent rows.

A *row* is a group of cells. The RTF expression of a row consists of a \trowd command, then a row declaration (which expresses the placement and borders of the cells), the cells themselves, and then the \row command. The parts between \trowd and \row are each made up of other, smaller parts.

In the minimal syntax we're discussing here, a row declaration consists of a \trgaph*Twips* command, followed by series of cell declarations. There are several ways of thinking about the \trgaph*Twips* command's meaning: one is that this number is half of the (minimal) gap between the content in adjacent cells (*trgaph* apparently stands for "Table, Row, Gap, Half"); the other way is to think of this number as the size of the "internal margin" in the cells. This distance is shown in Figure 17, labeled as "P".

Figure 17. Internal margins between cells

For example, consider a row with this structure:

```
\trowd \trgaph180
...cell declarations here...
...cells here...
\trow
```

This row has cells with internal margins of at least 180 twips—i.e., an eighth of an inch, or about 3 millimeters. That means that the content in adjacent cells would be at

---

least twice that far apart, namely 360 twips, a quarter of an inch, or about 6 millimeters.

Each cell declaration consists of at least a \cellx*TwipsReach* command, which declares the distance between the left margin and this cell's right end. Note that this isn't the width of each cell, but instead the offset of its rightmost extreme.

Cells are declared left to right, as you might expect.

Consider a row with these cell declarations:

```
\trowd \trgaph180
\cellx1440 \cellx2880 \cellx3600
...cells here...
\row
```

These declarations express that there are three cells in the row: the first (starting from the left) ends at 1,440 twips (1 inch) from the left margin; the second ends at 2,880 twips (2 inches) from the left margin; and the last one ends 3,600 twips (2 and a half inches) from the left margin.

Each cell is expressed as \pard\intbl ...\cell. For example, \pard\intbl stuff\cell expresses a cell that contains simply the word "stuff". If you want to start a new line in the middle of the text content, use the \line command instead of a \par command, as shown here:

```
\pard\intbl {\b The History Channel}
\line (Not available in Canada)\cell
```

It is also valid to have an empty cell. That would be expressed as just \pard\intbl\cell.

After the final cell in this row is a \row command.

A row must consist of one or more cells—a row with no cells at all is not allowed, and is one of the many invalid table constructs that can crash MSWord. The cell declaration must declare exactly as many cells as will actually follow in this row—do not declare five cells but have six, or vice versa.

Building Tables

Using the syntax explained above, the simplest case of a row is one with just one cell:

```
\trowd \trgaph180
\cellx1440
\pard\intbl Fee.\cell
\row
```

That comes out like this:

> Fee.

To make two cells, we add another \cellx*Rightreach* in the declaration, and then another \pard\intbl...\cell, as shown here:

```
\trowd \trgaph180
\cellx1440\cellx2880
\pard\intbl Fee.\cell
\pard\intbl Fie.\cell
\row
```

| Fee. | Fie. |

To make a "real" table, we just need two or more rows, one after the other:

```
\trowd \trgaph180
\cellx1440\cellx2880
\pard\intbl Fee.\cell
\pard\intbl Fie.\cell
\row

\trowd \trgaph180
\cellx1440\cellx2880
\pard\intbl Foe.\cell
\pard\intbl Fum.\cell
\row
```

| Fee. | Fie. |
| Foe. | Fum. |

Wrapping the parts of a table in {...} groups isn't necessary, but often helps for grouping things visually, as well as for preventing formatting commands from having "runaway"

---

effects—i.e., affecting more of the document than was intended. So the above code without any {...} groups is fine, but here's the same code with groups inserted just as an example of how to play it safe:

```
{
\trowd \trgaph180
\cellx1440\cellx2880
\pard\intbl {Fee.}\cell
\pard\intbl {Fie.}\cell
\row
}{
\trowd \trgaph180
\cellx1440\cellx2880
\pard\intbl {Foe.}\cell
\pard\intbl {Fum.}\cell
\row
}
```

The newlines (and the optional space after each command) are there just to make it easier for us humans to read the source. You can get exactly the same table by removing that whitespace in the source, like so:

```
\trowd\trgaph180\cellx1440\cellx2880\pard\intbl Fee.\cell
\pard\intbl Fie.\cell\row\trowd\trgaph180\cellx1440
\cellx2880\pard\intbl Foe.\cell\pard\intbl Fum.\cell\row
```

It's all the same to the program that's reading the RTF. But good luck debugging table code that has no helpful newlines or {...} groups in it!

Content that Stretches Rows

Most readers are familiar with HTML tables, but there is a basic difference between HTML tables and RTF tables. Consider the table that this HTML source expresses:

```
<table>
  <tr>  <td>Fee</td>  <td>Fie</td>  </tr>
  <tr>  <td>Foe</td>  <td>Fum</td>  </tr>
</table>
```

When a web browser lays out that HTML table, it makes each cell take up as much space as it needs, horizontally and vertically. That is, if you replace "Fum" with a longer phrase, the browser will use more horizontal space:

```
<table>
  <tr>  <td>Fee</td> <td>Fie</td>  </tr>
  <tr>  <td>Foe</td> <td>Fum -- and what on earth is a fum?</td>
  </tr>
</table>
```

Fee	Fie
Foe	Fum -- and what on earth is a fum?

Only if the browser runs out of horizontal space does it try using more vertical space by wrapping cell content onto another line. (For the sake of argument we're ignoring HTML constructs like <td width=123>.)

But an RTF table cell is fundamentally different: its declaration determines exactly how wide the cell will be; there is no allowance for it to be any other width. That means adding more content in a cell can only make it grow down:

```
\trowd \trgaph180
\cellx1440\cellx2880
\pard\intbl Fee.\cell
\pard\intbl Fie.\cell
\row

\trowd \trgaph180
\cellx1440\cellx2880
\pard\intbl Foe.\cell
\pard\intbl Fum -- and what on earth is a fum?\cell
\row
```

Fee.	Fie.
Foe.	Fum -- and what on earth is a fum?

In other words, when an RTF row is defined, its cells' widths are defined; the word processor takes care of figuring out how much height the content requires.

Starting Tables Away from the Left Margin

We have seen how a series of \cellx commands expresses the horizontal settings of cells by placing the right edge for each one. This may seem an odd way to do things—you might have wanted to declare the width of each cell instead—but it does work, and it's not hard to do a bit of addition and subtraction to convert a list of widths to a list of right edges. In fact, the one value that's not inherently expressed in a series of cellx values is the left edge of a table. For this edge, there is a separate command: \trleft*Twips* expresses the distance between the left margin on the left edge of the table. This command goes right after the \trgaph command. If \trleft*Twips* is missing, as it has been in our examples so far, it means the same as if it were present with a value of zero, \trleft0, meaning that the table starts right on the left margin.

For example, suppose we want a row with two cells, the first cell two and a half inches across, and the second cell an inch and a quarter across; and suppose that we want the table to start an inch and a half from the left margin, and to have an internal margin of an eighth of an inch. This is shown in Figure 18 (and yes, it is identical to Figure 17).

Figure 18. A row with two cells

Here are the values for those distances:

```
A:  1 1/2 "
B:  2 1/2 "
C:  1 1/4 "
P:    1/8 "
```

The first step is to convert the values to twips. Use the "Converting to Twips" section in Part IV for this, or just remember to multiply the value by 1,440 (if you're going from centimeters to twips, multiply by the memorable number 567):

```
A:   2160 twips
B:   3600 twips
C:   1800 twips
P:    180 twips
```

The P value for the internal margin on cells is what we'll plug into the \trgaph command at the start of the row declaration. Since that's the only place it needs to be expressed, we then delete it from our list of values. That leaves us with:

```
2160 twips
3600 twips
1800 twips
```

The last step is to turn this from widths to offsets, which we do by just keeping a running total, starting with 0.

Widths			Running total
2160 twips +	0	=	2160 twips
3600 twips +	2160	=	5760 twips
1800 twips +	5760	=	7560 twips

Take this list of running totals, 2160, 5760, 7560, and use the first as a \trleft value and the rest as \cellx values; that completes the row declaration, so we can finally add cell content (each cell in a \pard\intbl...\cell), and end the row with a \row. This is all shown in Figure 19.

Widths-to-Offsets as an Algorithm

Above, we expressed the very simple running total algorithm in informal terms. Here it is expressed as a Perl subroutine:

```perl
sub widths2offsets {
  my @widths = @_;
  my $total = 0;
  my @offsets;
  foreach my $w (@widths) {
    $total = $total + $w;
    push @offsets, $total;
  }
  return @offsets;
}
```

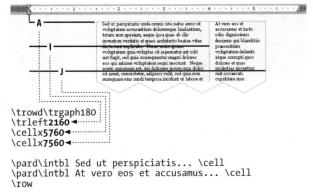

```
\trowd\trgaph180
\trleft2160
\cellx5760
\cellx7560

\pard\intbl Sed ut perspiciatis... \cell
\pard\intbl At vero eos et accusamus... \cell
\row
```

Figure 19. The widths within a row

Fans of terse code might prefer this, which does the same thing: sub widths2offsets { my $t; map(($t += $_), @_) }.

We can use that subroutine in code like this:

```
my @widths = ( 2160, 3600, 1800 );
my @offsets = widths2offsets( @widths );

print "Widths: @widths\nOffsets: @offsets\n";
print "\\trleft", shift( @offsets ), "\n";
foreach (@offsets) { print "\\cellx$_\n" }
```

Running the code produces this output, which shows that our math in the previous example was correct:

```
Widths: 2160 3600 1800
Offsets: 2160 5760 7560

\trleft2160
\cellx5760
\cellx7560
```

Adding Borders

The examples of formatted tables shown above are actually screenshots of tables with no real borders; the fine lines that seem to be borders are just shown for the sake of navigation.

That is, this table:

```
\trowd \trgaph180
\cellx1440\cellx2880
\pard\intbl Fee.\cell
\pard\intbl Fie.\cell
\row

\trowd \trgaph180
\cellx1440\cellx2880
\pard\intbl Foe.\cell
\pard\intbl Fum.\cell
\row
```

Looks like this on screen:

Fee.	Fie.
Foe.	Fum.

Printed out, it looks like this:

    Fee.   Fie.
    Foe.   Fum.

In order to add real borders, put this code before each \cellx*N*
command:

```
\clbrdrt\brdrw15\brdrs
\clbrdrl\brdrw15\brdrs
\clbrdrb\brdrw15\brdrs
\clbrdrr\brdrw15\brdrs
```

This construct turns on borders for each side of a given cell
being declared. Clearly, it makes for rather verbose RTF,
since adding borders to a two-cell table turns this:

```
\cellx1440\cellx2880
```

into this:

```
\clbrdrt\brdrw15\brdrs
\clbrdrl\brdrw15\brdrs
\clbrdrb\brdrw15\brdrs
\clbrdrr\brdrw15\brdrs\cellx1440
\clbrdrt\brdrw15\brdrs
\clbrdrl\brdrw15\brdrs
\clbrdrb\brdrw15\brdrs
\clbrdrr\brdrw15\brdrs\cellx2880
```

In that border code, the "15" in \brdrw15 expresses the width of the border, in twips (\brdrw for *border width*). You can replace this with any number, up to a maximum value of 75. Also, you can replace \brdrs (which means *border single*) with any of the 30 (!) different border commands that the RTF Specification lists in its section "Paragraph *[sic!]* Borders," of which these are the most notable:

```
\brdrs        Simple border
\brdrdot      Dotted border
\brdrdash     Dashed border
\brdrdb       Double border
```

To create a border-less cell, omit the \clbrdrt... construct before the \cellx command in its declaration

For example, this code defines a 2 x 2 table in which the top row has a 35-twip-wide dotted border (\brdrw35\brdrdot), and the bottom row has no border at all:

```
\trowd \trgaph180
\clbrdrt\brdrw35\brdrdot
\clbrdrl\brdrw35\brdrdot
\clbrdrb\brdrw35\brdrdot
\clbrdrr\brdrw35\brdrdot\cellx1440
\clbrdrt\brdrw35\brdrdot
\clbrdrl\brdrw35\brdrdot
\clbrdrb\brdrw35\brdrdot
\clbrdrr\brdrw35\brdrdot\cellx2880

\pard\intbl Fee.\cell  \pard\intbl Fie.\cell
\row

\trowd \trgaph180
\cellx1440\cellx2880
\pard\intbl Foe.\cell  \pard\intbl Fum.\cell
\row
```

It prints out like this:

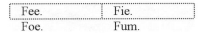

So far we've been treating this block as one giant construct:

```
\clbrdrt\brdrw15\brdrs
\clbrdrl\brdrw15\brdrs
\clbrdrb\brdrw15\brdrs
\clbrdrr\brdrw15\brdrs
```

But it's four occurrences of a `\`*`BorderDirection`*`\brdrw15\brdrs` idiom, in which there are four *BorderDirection* commands:

```
\clbrdrt : Cell Border Top
\clbrdrl : Cell Border Left
\clbrdrb : Cell Border Bottom
\clbrdrr : Cell Border Right
```

If you want only a top and bottom border on a cell, you would simply have:

```
\clbrdrt\brdrw15\brdrs
\clbrdrb\brdrw15\brdrs
```

Incidentally, a grammar for what we've been discussing can be expressed like this:

```
Row         := \trowd RowDecl RowCell+ \row
RowDecl     := \trgaphN? \trleft? CellDecl+
RowCell     := \pard\intbl TextContent \cell

CellDecl    := CellBorders \cellxN

CellBorders := DeclTop? DeclLeft? DeclBottom? DeclRight?
DeclTop     := \clbrdrt OneBorder
DeclLeft    := \clbrdrl OneBorder
DeclBottom  := \clbrdrb OneBorder
DeclRight   := \clbrdrr OneBorder
OneBorder   := \brdrwN BorderType
BorderType  := ( \brdrs | \brdrdot | \brdrdash | \brdrdb )
```

If you find formal grammars useful, have a look at the RTF Specification; it uses them a lot.

Vertical Alignment in Cells

When a word processor lays out content in a cell and finds that there is room left over on the top or the bottom, it has to add space to the top, or the bottom, or both. The word processor's decision for each cell is controlled by one of three commands inserted before the `\cellx` that declares that cell:

`\clvertalt\cellx`*Num*
    Align content with the top of the cell (usually the default).

`\clvertalc\cellx`*Num*
    Vertically center content in this cell.

`\clvertalb\cellx`*Num*
    Align content with the bottom of this cell.

Here's an example:

```
\trowd\trleft0\trgaph120
\cellx1440
\clvertalt\cellx2880
\clvertalc\cellx4320
\clvertalb\cellx5760
\pard\intbl {\fs50 Wise man say:}\cell
\pard\intbl {\i The large print giveth}\cell
\pard\intbl {\i and the small print}\cell
\pard\intbl {\i taketh away.}\cell
\row
```

Wise man say:	*The large print giveth*	*and the small print*	*taketh away.*

Horizontal Alignment in Cells

Given that there are the three special commands (\clvertalt, \clvertalc, and \clvertalb) for aligning things vertically in a table cell, you might expect another three commands specially for aligning things horizontally in a table cell. Instead, RTF does this by applying three general-purpose commands for paragraph justification: \ql, \qc, and \qr, to align to the left, center, or right. Left alignment is generally the default. Here's an example:

```
\trowd\trleft0\trgaph120\cellx1440
\cellx2880\cellx4320\cellx5760
\pard\intbl {\fs50 Wise man say:}\cell
\pard\intbl\ql {\i The large print giveth}\cell
\pard\intbl\qc {\i and the small print}\cell
\pard\intbl\qr {\i taketh away.}\cell
\row
```

Wise man say:	*The large print giveth*	*and the small print*	*taketh away.*

A caveat: it's a good idea to use braces around each cell's content (shown above) to keep formatting from bleeding over into subsequent cells. That is, if you had `\pard\intbl\i Hi!\cell`, the `\i` would apply to this cell and all subsequent cells! (Unless you started the other cells with a `\plain`.) That could be avoided by having `\pard\intbl{\i Hi!}\cell`. However, if you get into the good habit of using braces that way, note that if you want to add a `\ql`, `\qc`, or `\qr`, you should do it outside the braces, as shown in the above example. If you instead did `\pard\intbl{\qc\i...}\cell`, the `\qc` might get ignored. For some interpretations of the RTF spec, the effect of the `\qc` is only temporary and goes away once the `{...}` group ends, and so is no longer applicable once the `\cell` gets around to formatting the content.

Horizontal and Vertical Alignment in Cells

From a language-design perspective, you might note an odd asymmetry in RTF cell alignment: the commands for horizontal alignment in the cell (`\ql`, `\qc`, `\qr`) are used in the cell's content itself, while the commands for vertical alignment are used earlier on, in the row declaration.

In spite of the odd position of the commands, it's perfectly fine to use both vertical and horizontal alignments for a given cell. In fact, here's a table that shows all the permutations:

```
\trowd\trleft0\trgaph120\cellx1440
\clvertalt\cellx2880 \clvertalt\cellx4320 \clvertalt\cellx5760
\pard\intbl {\fs50 Wise man say:}\cell
\pard\intbl\ql {\i The large print giveth}\cell
\pard\intbl\qc {\i and the small print}\cell
\pard\intbl\qr {\i taketh away.}\cell
\row

\trowd\trleft0\trgaph120\cellx1440
\clvertalc\cellx2880 \clvertalc\cellx4320 \clvertalc\cellx5760
\pard\intbl {\fs50 Wise man say:}\cell
\pard\intbl\ql {\i The large print giveth}\cell
\pard\intbl\qc {\i and the small print}\cell
\pard\intbl\qr {\i taketh away.}\cell
\row

\trowd\trleft0\trgaph120\cellx1440
\clvertalb\cellx2880 \clvertalb\cellx4320 \clvertalb\cellx5760
\pard\intbl {\fs50 Wise man say:}\cell
```

```
\pard\intbl\ql {\i The large print giveth}\cell
\pard\intbl\qc {\i and the small print}\cell
\pard\intbl\qr {\i taketh away.}\cell
\row
```

Wise man say:	*The large print giveth*	*and the small print*	*taketh away.*
Wise man say:	*The large print giveth*	*and the small print*	*taketh away.*
Wise man say:	*The large print giveth*	*and the small print*	*taketh away.*

The default alignment for a table cell is generally as is shown in the topmost "The large print giveth" cell: vertically aligned to the top, and horizontally aligned to the left.

The table happens to have no borders declared, but that's just to avoid having the RTF code take up even more paper! It's perfectly valid to use borders along with alignment commands.

If you still have our formal grammar in mind from a few pages ago, consider that these new rules amend the grammar to allow for the alignment commands that we've been talking about:

```
CellDecl   := CellBorders CellVAlign? \cellxN
RowCell    := \pard\intbl CellHAlign? TextContent \cell
CellHAlign := ( \ql | \qc | \qr )
CellVAlign := ( \clvertalt | \clvertalc | \clvertalb )
```

Creating MS Windows Help Files

Part II contains information about generating MSWindows help files (*.HLP*), which can be read on any machine with MSWindows.

MSWindows help files are generated using the Microsoft Help Compiler (*hc.exe*), which can be downloaded free at *ftp://ftp.microsoft.com/Softlib/MSLFILES/HC505.EXE*. There are other utilities in that directory that generate help files, notably *HCWSETUP.EXE* and *WHAT6.EXE*, which differ mainly in their interface.

The Microsoft Help Compiler needs its input to be in RTF— but not just any kind of RTF. It uses a dialect of RTF that adds some RTF commands, doesn't support other RTF commands, and changes the meaning of a few more RTF commands. Part II describes how to write simple RTF to produce a no-frills *.HLP* file, but does not go into the fancier features of Help-RTF.

Help-RTF Basics

A Help-RTF file starts as basic RTF, but contains a list of *topics*. A topic consists of paragraphs preceded by a topic definition, and followed by a \page command. Informally, I'll also refer to topics as *screens* or *topic-screens*.

A topic definition is a bunch of lines that give the help compiler some metadata about the screen. Strangely, the \footnote command is used for each part. A topic definition consists minimally of this syntax:

```
#{\footnote context_string}
```

in which *context_string* is a unique string that can be used as this particular topic-screen's URL. The string must not contain spaces; it should consist of just characters from the set A–Z, 0–9, period, and underscore. Lowercase letters can be used, but case is not significant. It would be nice if Microsoft had called these "screen IDs" or something a bit more self-evident than "context-strings"; but "context string" is indeed the term that you will see if, for example, Help Compiler emits an error message like "Invalid context string 'main-screen'."

For example, this code defines a topic that has the context string identifier "Main_screen", then consists of just a paragraph offering some helpful advice, and ends the topic.

```
#{\footnote Main_screen}
{\pard\plain
When in panic or in doubt, run in circles,
 scream, and shout.
\par}
\page
```

To build a *.HLP* file that consists just of that one screen, wrap it in some basic RTF:

```
{\rtf1\ansi\deff0
{\fonttbl {\f0\froman Times New Roman;}}
\deflang1033\plain

#{\footnote Main_screen}
{\pard\plain
When in panic or in doubt, run in circles,
 scream, and shout.
\par}
\page

}
```

Save that in a file called *scream.rtf*, then create a file called *scream.hpj* consisting of these lines:

```
[OPTIONS]
ERRORLOG=HELP.LOG
REPORT=ON
CONTENTS=Main_screen
  ; that's the context_string of the main screen
TITLE=Wise Advice
  ; or whatever you want the window-title to be
```

```
[FILES]
scream.rtf

[CONFIG]
BrowseButtons()
```

Then just run *hc scream* and you should see something like:

```
c:\stuff>hc scream.hpj
Microsoft (R) Help Compiler Version 3.10.505
Copyright (c) Microsoft Corp 1990 - 1992. All rights reserved.
scream.HPJ

Compiling file scream.rtf.
Resolving context strings.
Resolving keywords.
```

Now there should be a *scream.hlp* file that can be opened by double-clicking or by running *winhelp scream.hlp* at a DOS prompt. Figure 20 shows the result.

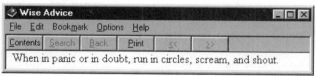

Figure 20. scream.hlp

Hyperlinks and Popups

A one-screen help file isn't much use. To get more screens, just have several #{\footnote *Context_string*}...\page sections in a document, like so:

```
{\rtf1\ansi\deff0
{\fonttbl {\f0\froman Times New Roman;}}
\deflang1033\plain

#{\footnote Main_screen}
{\pard\plain
When in panic or in doubt, run in circles,
 scream, and shout.
\par}
\page

#{\footnote Panic_screen}
```

```
{\pard\plain
Panic is the technical term
 for {\b\i freaking out!}
\par}
\page

}
```

However, when you compile and open that help file, you'll see the Main_screen screen (since that's what *scream.hpj* declared as this document's start-screen), but there's no way to get to the other screen, "Panic_screen". That's what hyperlinks are for. Here's how to make a link to another screen:

```
{\uldb text to display}{\v Context_string}
```

That's the Help-RTF equivalent of `<a href="url">text to display</a>` in HTML.

Make the word "panic" on the first screen into a link to the second screen (whose content string is "Panic_screen"):

```
#{\footnote Main_screen}
{\pard\plain
When in {\uldb panic}{\v Panic_screen}
 or in doubt, run in circles,
 scream, and shout.
\par}
\page
```

Figure 21 shows the main screen. Clicking on the underlined word "panic" brings you to the Panic_screen, shown in Figure 22.

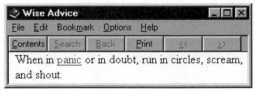

Figure 21. Showing a simple hyperlink

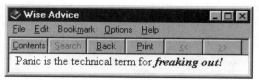

Figure 22. The result of following the hyperlink

There is another way to do Help-RTF hyperlinks, so that the screen you're targeting appears in a little popup when the link is clicked (instead of replacing the current window). You get this by changing the \uldb to a \ul, like so:

```
{\ul text to display}{\v Context_string}
```

As in:

```
{\pard\plain
When in {\ul panic}{\v Panic_screen}
 or in doubt, run in circles,
 scream, and shout.
\par}
\page
```

This looks about the same as before, until the link is selected—then it looks like this Figure 23.

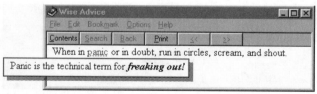

Figure 23. Activating a popup link

Notice that popup links have a dotted underline, while normal links have a solid underline.

More Topic Information

So far we've been using just #{\footnote Context_string} to start a topic. That's the minimum needed, but there are other optional but useful features worth mentioning. The full syntax for starting a topic is:

```
#{\footnote Context_string}
${\footnote Actual visible title}
K{\footnote ;First keyword; Second keyword; ...;}
+{\footnote browse-group:number}
```

For example:

```
#{\footnote Panic_screen}
${\footnote Everything You Ever Wanted To Know About Panicking}
K{\footnote ;Panic;Freak-outs;Hysteria}
+{\footnote Main:0020}
```

The first group, #{\footnote Context_string}, defines the context-string for making links to this screen. The second group, ${\footnote Actual visible title}, sets the visible title for this page. That title isn't visible when you're viewing the page (so you typically want to duplicate it as a heading at the start of the screen), but it shows up in the history subwindow (see Figure 24), and in the search screens when they display a link to the page (see Figure 25).

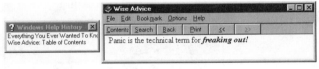

Figure 24. A history subwindow

The last search screen, Figure 26, shows all keywords (a.k.a. index terms) in the document; double-clicking on one will bring up the screen that is indexed under that keyword (or if there are several screens, a menu for picking which one to bring up). But this only works for whatever screens have keywords defined for them. The way to define keyword(s) for a screen is to use the K-footnote construction:

```
K{\footnote ;First keyword; Second keyword; ...;}
```

Each keyword (or keyphrase, actually, as it can be several words), is delimited by semicolons. There can also be space around each semicolon.

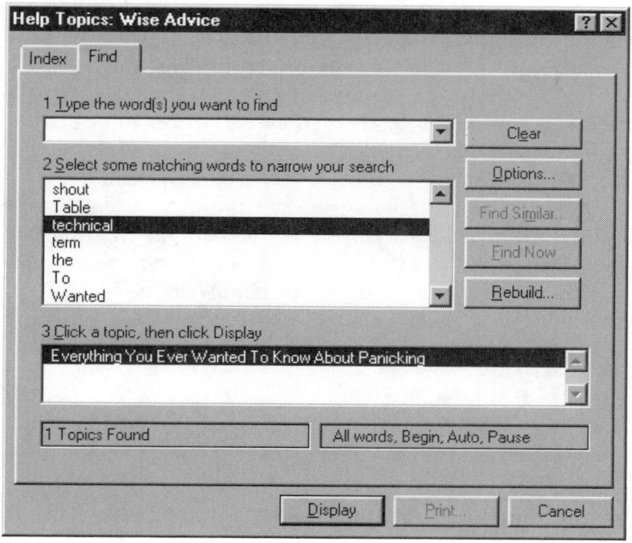

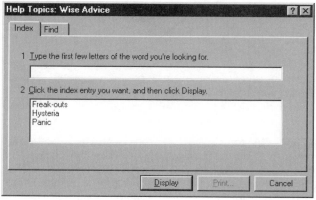

Figure 25. The Help Topics "Find" window

Figure 26. Help Topics "Index" window

You may have noticed the greyed-out "<<" and ">>" keys on the button-bar of the figures so far. This is where browse-sequences come in. The final \footnote construction is +{\ footnote *browse-group:number*}. If you have +{\footnote *browse-group:number*} constructions on at least some of your screens, the Help Compiler takes them and groups together the ones with the same browse-group string. Then, the Help Compiler ASCIIbetically sorts each group according to its number (which can actually be any alphanumeric string, but for sanity's sake you should stick to 4-digit numbers, incremented by tens, like 0010, 0020, etc.). Then the Help Compiler makes the "<<" and ">>" buttons go back and forth among the sorted screens in each group.

Suppose you have seven topic-screens, with these browse-sequence strings and titles:

Browse-sequence string	Title
Main:0010	Table of Contents
Main:0020	Purpose
Main:0030	Basic concepts
Main:0040	Examples
Ref:0010	Function reference
Ref:0020	Variable reference
Ref:0030	Operator reference
[none]	About the Author
[none]	License

These are shown sorted first by the browse-group, then the browse-number; it doesn't matter in what order the RTF source file defines the topic-screens. Also, the browse-sequence strings aren't visible to the user.

In any case, among the above topic-screens, the Main:0010 screen ("Table of Contents") will have a ">>" link to the Main:0020 screen ("Purpose"), which will have a "<<" link back to Main:0010 and a ">>" link forward to Main:0020 ("Basic concepts"). Similarly, Main:0030 will back link to Main:0020 and forward to Main:0040. But Main:0040 does not link to Ref:0010, because they are in different browse groups. And in the Ref group, there are forward and back links between the topic-screens, just as within the Main group.

As for the "About the Author" topic-screen and the "License" topic-screen, they are not part of any browse-group (i.e., they lack a +{\footnote *anything*} definition). The "<<" and ">>" buttons will be greyed out on those screens.

You don't have to define several browse groups: you can have all your browse-sequence strings be of the form Main: *somenumber*.

If you don't have a +{\footnote *anything*} definition string on any of the topic-screens in your document, the "<<" and ">>" buttons will never be useful, and can be hidden. Alter the *filename.hpj* by deleting this line:

```
BrowseButtons()
```

Or add a ";" at the start of the line, which comments it out.

Images

While embedding images in normal RTF is agonizing, it is simple in Help-RTF, even if the idiom looks a bit odd:

```
{\'7b
bmc filename.bmp
\'7d}
```

This code inserts the graphic from the file *filename.bmp* at the current point, as a character. That is, just inserting a new graphic with that code does not, by itself, start a new line.

For example, consider this code:

```
{\pard\plain If you scream too much -- like
 {\'7b
bmc panic.bmp
\'7d}
 -- then you'll go hoarse!
\par}
```

It displays as if the *panic.bmp* image were one very, very tall character; see Figure 27.

Figure 27. An image displayed as an inline character

If you want the image to display without text on either side, make it a paragraph by itself, especially one that uses the \sb and \sa codes to set itself off from the previous paragraphs, and a \qc to center the image:

```
{\pard\sa240\qc\plain\f1\fs30\b\i All About Screaming\par}
{\pard\plain This is what screaming looks like: \par}

{\pard\qc\sb180\sa180
{\'7b
bmc panic.bmp
\'7d}
\par}

{\pard\plain If you look like that and are making a loud
  noise, then you're screaming.\par}
```

That will look like Figure 28.

Image files have to be BMPs—Help Compiler doesn't accept GIFs, JPEGs, etc. Moreover, the current version of Help Compiler still doesn't understand MSWindows "long" file-names, so if you use a file called *hysterical.bmp*, you won't be

Figure 28. An image displayed as its own centered paragraph

able to include it with a {\'7bbmc hysterical.bmp\'7d} construct, because Help Compiler tries to find *hysteric.bmp*, fails, and produces an error message. You have three choices in this case:

- Name your files with a maximum of eight characters before the ".bmp" suffix. That avoids the problem altogether.

- Use the more recent help-file compiler, Microsoft Help Workshop. It's the GUI equivalent to the command-line Help Compiler (and contains a program called *hcrtf* that is basically a replacement for Help Compiler, although its command-line syntax is more baroque). A notable feature of Help Workshop is that it understands long filenames.

The program is available at *ftp://ftp.microsoft.com/Softlib/ MSLFILES/HCWSETUP.EXE*. Quite fittingly, its help file comes with a wealth of reference information on many details of Help-RTF, as well as instructions on how to work the program.

- If you do want to use Help Compiler to include a file with a long name, use `dir` *longfilename* from an MSDOS window. For example, the long filename *hysterical.bmp* probably has *hyster~1.bmp* as its short filename equivalent. So you would just use {\'7bbmc hyster~1.bmp\'7d} in your RTF.

Other ways to get the short filename are to run

```
perl -e "print Win32::GetShortPathName(shift)" longfilename
```

at an MSDOS prompt (assuming you have ActiveState Perl installed); or, in a Windows Explorer window, select "File: Properties" and look at the "MS-DOS name" field.

Help-RTF's Peculiarities

The Help Compiler is, at times, finicky about the kinds of RTF accepts. Ideally, Help-RTF would just be normal RTF with all the document content wrapped in #{\footnote *Context_string*}...\page sections. But in practice, some RTF constructs must be avoided; some RTF features (notably tables) are only partially supported; and you may discover that some constructs that are optional in normal RTF are basically required in Help-RTF.

Most such problems with Help-RTF can be avoided by using this as the start of your document:

```
{\rtf1\ansi\deff0
{\fonttbl
{\f0\froman Times New Roman;}
{\f1\fswiss Arial;}
{\f2\fmodern Courier New;}
}
\deflang1033\plain
```

Feel free to replace the "1033" (which means U.S.-English) with the appropriate language code, as listed in Part IV in the section "RTF Language Codes."

In theory, you could use different fonts than the above "standard" fonts; but by sticking to the standard fonts, you can be sure that the resulting .*HLP* file will be readable on any MSWindows machine.

In addition, these RTF commands have different meanings in Help-RTF: \footnote, \keep, \keepn, \page, \strike, \trqc, \ul, \uldb, \v. We discussed only some of them in this book. For a full discussion of each command's new meaning in Help-RTF, refer to the Microsoft documentation that comes with Help Workshop. A good rule of thumb is to avoid any of those commands, except in the constructs previously discussed.

Learning More

Even if you choose to stick with trusty old Microsoft Help Compiler for compiling your help files, I suggest downloading Microsoft Help Workshop (its URL is mentioned above), if only for its thorough documentation on Help-RTF's more arcane features. For general information on producing MS Windows help files, see *http://helpmaster.com*. Finally, I highly recommend the commercial program RoboHelp for automating the composition (not just the compilation) of help files. Product information on RoboHelp can be found at *http://www.ehelp.com/products/robohelp/*.

## PART III

Example Programs

So far, this book has approached RTF as a format that means something in and of itself. But RTF, like any document format, makes sense only in terms of how it is used—namely, how it is formatted and read. The issue of parsing RTF is larger than can be dealt with in this brief guide, but these simple RTF-generating programs demonstrate the basic issues involved in having programs that write RTF documents. The examples are of simple utilities that each use some particular features of RTF.

The programs are all in relatively simple Perl, with an explanation before each, and comments in the code. If you want to generate your own RTF documents from Perl, have a look at the helpful RTF-writing modules in CPAN (located at *http://search.cpan.org*), notably RTF::Writer and RTF::Generator. I don't actually use these modules in the following examples, because the examples simply demonstrate RTF without detouring through the APIs of the RTF-writing modules.

A Datebook Generator

This program starts a new RTF file, writes an RTF prolog, writes a series of paragraphs (one at a time, in each pass through the while loop), and then closes the document with a single } character. Each paragraph that it writes is a heading for each day's worth of space in a datebook (which can be printed out and bound, so you have someplace to pencil in notes about upcoming appointments, deadlines, brunches, court dates, box socials, and the like). You can get a blank space between the paragraphs by using the \sa (space after) command with some relatively large values.

Lines in the file look like this:

```
...
{\pard\sa6060\qr\f0{\b Friday,} 28{\super th} of November, 2003\par}
{\pard\sa2900\qr\f0{\b Saturday,} 29{\super th} of November, 2003\par}
{\pard\sa2900\qr\f0{\b Sunday,} 30{\super th} of November, 2003\par}
{\pard\sa6060\qr\f1{\b Monday,} 1{\super st} of December, 2003\par}
{\pard\sa6060\qr\f1{\b Tuesday,} 2{\super nd} of December, 2003\par}
{\pard\sa6060\qr\f1{\b Wednesday,} 3{\super rd} of December, 2003\par}
{\pard\sa6060\qr\f1{\b Thursday,} 4{\super th} of December, 2003\par}
...
```

The paragraphs vary: note that Saturday and Sunday get less space (only 2,900 twips instead of 6,060 twips). This detail is controlled by the $space variable in the program, as it is set to either the constant DAY_BIG or DAY_SMALL, depending on the $weekday variable. Moreover, the font alternates depending on the month. This is done by adding the result of *monthnumber* % 2 to \f, where % is the Perl "modulus" operator. Of course, the font table controls exactly what fonts \f0 and \f1 actually produce. Figure 29 shows the sample pages.

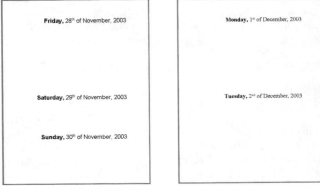

Figure 29. Datebook sample pages

There are two subtle problems with this program, which cause no trouble in the program as it is, but could appear as changes are implemented.

The first potential problem is that the strings we're inserting into the RTF document aren't being passed through an escaper routine. It happens to be okay, because none of the strings in the program need escaping (they're not \, {, }, or 8-bit characters). But imagine that you were changing this program to print the dates in Spanish; you would fill in the Spanish month names and weekday names, and slightly change the printf line. The output would include lines like this:

```
{\pard\sa6060\qr\f1{\b Miércoles}, el 3 diciembre, 2003\par}
```

Most word processors would reject a document containing that line, because it contains a raw é character. Since that's an 8-bit character, it should have been escaped (as \'e9), as explained at the beginning of Part III.

The other potential problem with this code is that it drops in some numeric values without checking that they're integers. It so happens that earlier on they were defined as numbers that are obviously integers (6,060 and 2,900). But suppose you adapted this program to a different paper size (currently the spacing is set to print on U.S. letter paper). And imagine that you wanted the big day-spaces to be 10cm, and the small day-spaces to be half of that.

So you'd look up 10cm in "Converting to Twips," see that 10cm is 5,669 twips, and make the code like this:

```
use constant DAY_BIG   => 5669;
use constant DAY_SMALL => DAY_BIG / 2; # half that
```

The problem arises when DAY_SMALL ends up being 2,834.5, and gives you code like this:

```
{\pard\sa5669\qr\f0{\b Friday,} 28{\super th} of November, 2003\par}
{\pard\sa2834.5\qr\f0{\b Saturday,} 29{\super th} of November,
2003\par}
{\pard\sa2834.5\qr\f0{\b Sunday,} 30{\super th} of November, 2003\par}
{\pard\sa5669\qr\f1{\b Monday,} 1{\super st} of December, 2003\par}
```

That isn't what you want. Because RTF keywords only take integer values, \sa2834.5 will be parsed as \sa2834 (i.e., the sa command, with an argument of 2,834) followed by the 2 literal characters ".5". So you will see headings ".5Saturday, 29th of November, 2003" and ".5Sunday, 30th of November, 2003." All numbers that are meant to be used as parameters in an RTF command should be made into integers—something that most computer languages (like Perl) do with an int command, like this:

```
printf RTF
  '{\pard\sa%s\qr\f%s{\b %s,} %s{\super %s} of %s, %s\par}' . "\n",
  int($space),
  int($month % 2),
```

The second int is actually redundant because the Perl % operator is documented as *always* returning an integer value—but it never hurts to be explicit.

Programmers at home with (s)printf formats may realize that the same thing could be accomplished by using a %d format (decimal-expressed integer), which does the work of int:

```
printf RTF
  '{\pard\sa%d\qr\f%d{\b %s,} %s{\super %s} of %s, %s\par}' . "\n",
  $space,
  $month % 2,
```

This option works just as well as the previous one. Which you choose depends on personal preference.

Finally, this program's basic approach to RTF-generation can be adapted to print flashcards instead of a datebook. If you print the document double-sided, then instead of printing two dates on one side of the page and two dates on the other, you could have a program print flashcard prompts on one side (for example, "buscar" and "escribir"), and the corresponding flashcard answers on the other side (for example, "to look for" and "to write"). Tear the page in half, and you have two flashcards. Such a flashcard-generator program could take its input from a file consisting of lines like buscar=to look for, and escribir=to write.

```
#!/usr/bin/perl
require 5;
use strict;
```

```perl
use warnings;
# (Run under a sane version of Perl, with optimal error-checking)

# Define some constants:
use constant SECONDS_IN_DAY => 24 * 60 * 60;
use constant DAY_BIG   => 6060; # twips
use constant DAY_SMALL => 2900; # twips

# Open the file and write the prolog
open RTF, ">datebook.rtf" or die $!;
print RTF '{\rtf1\ansi\deff0
{\fonttbl{\f0\fswiss Arial;}{\f1\froman Times New Roman;}}
\deflang1033\plain\fs50
';

# Define our lookup arrays of the names
# of the months and the days of the week
my @months = qw(
 January February March     April   May      June
 July    August  September  October November December
);
my @dows  = qw(
 Sunday Monday Tuesday Wednesday Thursday Friday Saturday
);

# start the datebook today, and end it a year from today
my $then = time();
my $end = $then + 366 * SECONDS_IN_DAY;

while($then <= $end) {
  my($year,$month,$day, $weekday) = (gmtime($then))[5,4,3,6];
  my $space = DAY_BIG;
  $space    = DAY_SMALL if $weekday == 0 or $weekday == 6;

  printf RTF
   '{\pard\sa%s\qr\f%s{\b %s,} %s{\super %s} of %s, %s\par}' . "\n",
    $space,
    $month % 2, # toggle the font every month
    $dows[$weekday], $day, th($day), $months[$month], $year + 1900,
  ;

  $then += SECONDS_IN_DAY;
}

# end and close the file, and quit the program
print RTF "}";
close(RTF);
exit;


sub th {
  # This is just a function to return the correct ordinal
  #  suffix, like 3 => "rd", so we don't say "February 3th"!
```

```
    my $n = abs($_[0] || 0);
    return 'th' unless $n and $n == int($n);
    $n %= 100;
    return 'th' if $n == 11 or $n == 12 or $n == 13;
    $n %= 10;
    return 'st' if $n == 1;
    return 'nd' if $n == 2;
    return 'rd' if $n == 3;
    return 'th';
}

__END__
```

A Directory Lister

This program reads a specified directory (or the current directory, if none is specified), and creates a directory listing in RTF, laid out using RTF tables. It's a fancy version of Unix `ls -l` or MSDOS `dir`.

This program's top-level flow structure is simple: when the program starts up, it checks for a command-line argument (in `$ARGV[0]`), looks up the current directory if it needs to, calls three subroutines (`rtf_start`, `rtfdir`, and `rtf_end`), and then quits.

The actual table generation code is in the `file_row` function. That function takes a file size, a filename, and a file's modification date, and formats them in a 3-row table cell. For example, a row that reads "24,544", "clip 1.gif", and "2003-03-23 03:07" is expressed by this monolith of RTF code:

```
\trowd\trgaph90\clbrdrt\brdrw15\brdrs\clbrdrb\brdrw15
\brdrs\clbrdrl\brdrw15\brdrs\clbrdrr\brdrw15\brdrs\cellx1224
\clbrdrt\brdrw15\brdrs\clbrdrb\brdrw15\brdrs\clbrdrl\brdrw15
\brdrs\clbrdrr\brdrw15\brdrs\cellx6120
\clbrdrt\brdrw15\brdrs\clbrdrb\brdrw15\brdrs\clbrdrl\brdrw15
\brdrs\clbrdrr\brdrw15\brdrs\cellx8280
\pard\intbl\qr{\fs18\f1\b 24,544}\cell
\ql{\f2 clip 1.gif}\cell
\qc{\fs18 2003-03-23 03\'3a07}\cell \row
```

Hopefully, the unavoidable ugliness of that RTF output is redeemed by the fact that its production is hidden behind a tidy function call: `file_row(name, size, modtime)`. The meaning of those commands is explained in detail in the "Tables" section of Part I.

The esc, in, and cm routines are quite re-useable in programs of your own. The esc routine implements a simple RTF escaper as discussed at the beginning of Part III; and in and cm are useful when you want to specify RTF distances in familiar units (inches or centimeters) instead of twips. You can see them used in file_row, where \cellx*RightEnd* commands are created based on the list in(.85), in(4.25), in(5.75) (which can be read as "point eight five inches," and so on). That is presumably friendlier than the list 1224, 6120, 8280, which is what those measurements work out to.

Naturally, whether you happen to choose to express distances as in(...) or cm(...) is simply a matter of which units you are most at home with; in the end, they are all converted to an integral number of twips. You can compare this approach to the discussion of int use in the previous RTF-writer program example.

The program reads as follows:

```perl
#!/usr/bin/perl
require 5;
use strict;
use warnings;
# (Run under a sane version of Perl, with optimal error-checking)

my $dir = $ARGV[0] || '.';
 # If there's no command line argument, then list the
 # contents of the current directory

if($dir eq '.' or $dir eq './') {
  use Cwd; # load the getcwd function's library
  $dir = getcwd();
  # So we can show the full path, instead of just "."
}

# Abort unless we're looking at a real live directory!
die "$dir isn't an existing readable directory"
 unless -e $dir and -d _ and -r _;

# Call our routines to do all the work, then quit:
rtf_start( $dir );
rtfdir( $dir );
rtf_end( $dir );
exit;
```

```
#-----------------------------------------------------------
# Three utility routines:

sub in { int(1440 * $_[0]) } #       inches -> twips

sub cm { int( 567 * $_[0]) } # centimeters -> twips

sub esc {  # return the given string, escaped as good RTF
  my $in = $_[0];
  $in =~ s{([^-"'?,\$\._a-zA-Z0-9 ])}
          {sprintf("\\'%02x",ord($1))}eg;
   # Actually escapes much more than is necessary, but
   # doesn't handle Unicode -- see Appendix A.
  return $in;
}
#-----------------------------------------------------------

# Declare three global variables for storing file data:
my( @Items, %Size_of, %Time_of );

sub rtfdir {             # do the main work of the program
  my $dir = $_[0];
  scan_dir($dir); # get the data

  print '{\pard\sa200\qc \fs50\b\i ', esc($dir), ' \par}', "\n\n";
   # page heading: the directory name

  file_row($_, $Size_of{$_}, $Time_of{$_} ) foreach @Items;
   # a row for every file

  print '{\pard\sb1440\sa1440\fs28\b\i [Empty!]}' unless @Items;

  return;
}

#-----------------------------------------------------------

sub scan_dir {
  # Gather the data for the files
  #   (this is used by the rtfdir function )
  # It's Just some dull filesystem functions here.
  #
  my $dir = $_[0];
  opendir(IN, $dir) or die "Can't opendir $dir: $!";
  my( $item, $full_path );

  while(defined( $item = readdir(IN) )) {
    next if $item eq '.' or $item eq '..';
    push @Items, $item;
    ( $Size_of{$item}, $Time_of{$item} ) = (-1,-1);
```

```perl
  my $full_path = "$dir/$item";
  ( $Size_of{$item}, $Time_of{$item} ) = ( stat($full_path) )[7,9]
   if -f $full_path;
  }

  closedir(IN);
  @Items = sort by_name @Items;
   # You can change "by_name" to "by_time" or "by_size"
  return;
}

# three ways to sort:
sub by_name { use locale; uc($a) cmp uc($b) }
sub by_time { $Time_of{$a} <=> $Time_of{$b} }
sub by_size { $Size_of{$a} <=> $Size_of{$b} }

#-----------------------------------------------------------

sub file_row {
  # Generate a table row for a file+size+time
  #  (used by the rtfdir function)

  my($name, $size, $time) = @_;
  my $name_format = '';
  if($size == -1) { # Our flag for a directory
    $name_format = '\b '; # make it bold
    $time = '';
    $size = '';

  } else { # It's a file...
    $time = format_date($time);
    1 while $size =~ s/(\d)(\d\d\d(,|$))/$1,$2/
     # Add commas to the size: 12345 => "12,345"
  }

  print '\trowd\trgaph90'; # Start the RTF row declaration
  my $borders = join "", map '\clbrdr' . $_ . '\brdrw15\brdrs',
   qw(t b l r); # turn on these borders (top bottom left right)

  print $borders, '\cellx', $_, "\n"
    for in(.85), in(4.25), in(5.75);  # declare the right ends
     # change these numbers as you like

  print   # emit the real cells and their content now:
   '\pard\intbl\qr{\fs18\f1\b ', esc($size) ,'}\cell ',
   # right-align, 9pt Courier bold
   '\ql{\f2 ', $name_format, esc($name), '}\cell ',
   # left-align Times Roman
   '\qc{\fs18 ', esc($time), '}\cell ',
   # centered 9pt Arial
   '\row', "\n\n"
  ;
```

```perl
    return;
  }

#-----------------------------------------------------------

sub rtf_start {
  my $dir = $_[0];
  print <<'END_RTF_START';
{\rtf1\ansi\deff0
{\fonttbl {\f0\fswiss Arial;}{\f1\fmodern Courier New;}
{\f2\froman Times;}}
\deflang1024\widowctrl\plain\fs24\noproof

END_RTF_START

  # Page header mentioning the path and time:
  print '{\header \pard\qr\plain\f0\fs18\i\noproof ',
    esc($dir . ' ' . format_date(time)),
    ' - p\chpgn\par}', "\n\n";
  return;
}

sub rtf_end {
  my $dir = $_[0];
  print "\n}\n";
  return;
}

sub format_date {
  my $time = $_[0];
  my($Y,$M,$D,$h,$m) = ( localtime( $time ) )[ 5,4,3,2,1 ];
  return sprintf "%04d-%02d-%02d %02d:%02d", $Y+1900, $M+1, $D,
$h,$m;
}

__END__
```

Just for sake of demonstration, this program doesn't open a new file and write RTF code to it—it simply sends RTF to standard output, which you can redirect at the shell prompt. Here is an example in MSWindows:

```
C:\> perl -S rtfdir.pl "\windows\desktop\symbol font table" >
%TEMP%\dir.rtf

C:\> start %TEMP%\dir.rtf
```

Figure 30 shows the resulting window in MSWord.

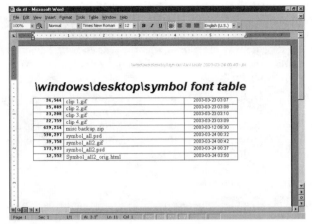

Figure 30. rtfdir output as viewed in MSWord

An Origami CD Case Maker

This program generates a single page that, when folded correctly, makes a CD case. Such cases are quite useful for all the CDRs that always manage to outnumber available plastic CD cases.*

This program begins by accepting lines of text to print on a label. Then it generates an RTF file with the text placed at a precise location on the page, along with lines that mark the folds. (Refer to the series of illustrations to see in which direction to fold in, and in what order to make the folds.)

The program uses two advanced RTF features: exact paragraph placement and line-drawing.

---

* Many thanks go to Tom Hull from the math department at Merrimack College for the original fold design. There's more information at *http://web.merrimack.edu/hullt/* and *http://papercdcase.com/*.

Position the text with \pvpg\phpg \posx*N* \posy*N* \absw*N* \absh*N* commands, as explained in the "Exact Paragraph Positioning" section of Part I. Without exact positioning of the paragraph, there'd be no way of assuring that the text ends up being visible, once the page is folded. This is also the approach to use with printing text on label-paper or envelopes.

Incidentally, the \absh-*ExactHeight* command makes sure that even if the user supplies more text than can fit, the program will hide whatever doesn't fit. Moreover, the text that the user provides is fed through the esc routine. So, for example, if the user enters fichiers non-analysées (French for "unanalyzed files"), that will correctly be escaped as fichiers non-analys\'e9s.

The line-drawing construct used in this program is a more elaborate version of what we saw in the "Line Drawing" section of Part I. Generating the RTF for a line from one point to another is more complex than just interpolating the two *(x,y)* pairs into a line of RTF—there is a bit of math involved. So we wrap all the necessary code in a subroutine, line, which we call whenever we need to draw lines.

Figure 31 shows what a file generated by this program looks like.

Some simpler text editors don't understand advanced features like paragraph positioning and line drawing. These text editors understand only the text in the generated file. Figure 32 shows how the document shows up in TextEdit, a simple text editor that comes with Mac OS X.

A conspicuous feature of the program is that we don't place lines with explicit numbers, like line(0, 11880, 12240, 11880). Instead, we do it with expressions like line(0, Page_Height*3/4, Page_Width, Page_Height*3/4). There's two reasons for this: using an expression like Page_Height*3/4 instead of 11,880 makes the geometric reasoning that gets us the number clear (although much of it isn't clear until you fold the page, and then unfold it and consider the geometry

---

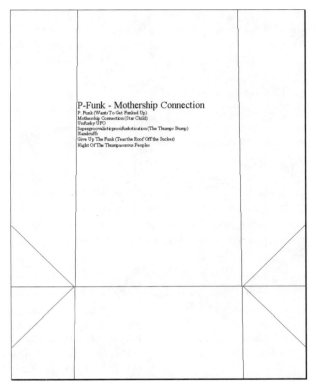

Figure 31. Origami CD case

of the folds). The other reason is more practical: all the numbers must change for a page that will be printed on A4 paper instead of U.S. letter paper, and the changes aren't arbitrary. They follow directly from the dimensions of the page, in a way that the expression Page_Height*3/4 captures perfectly.

The program can take input from a file, as with:

```
% cdcase title_and_tracklist.txt
```

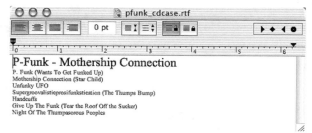

Figure 32. The document as seen in TextEdit

Or it can take input from standard input, e.g.:

```
% cdcase < title_and_tracklist.txt
```

Or:

```
% ls -l ./backups5 | cdcase
```

Or it can just read input from the console:

```
% cdcase
Enter text for CD case, then hit Enter and EOF (control-z)
The CD Title
Title for track 1
Title for track 2
Title for track 3
[then hit control-D or control-Z on a new line]
```

In any case, unless you hit break (typically Control-c), the program will write the CD case to the file *cd_case.rtf*. If no input is provided, the program writes a blank case: a page with no text, but with all the fold lines. You can open that file in a word processor and edit it to have whatever text you like, before printing it, folding it up (as shown in Figures 33 through 36), and using it. Here is the program:

```
#!/usr/bin/perl
require 5;
use strict;
use warnings;
# (Run under a sane version of Perl, with optimal error-checking)

#-----------------------------------------------------------
# Declare some constants:
```

Hardcopy a CD case from the program. Don't use thick paper (the paper won't hold the creases.) Normal printer paper is just fine.

Flip the page over so that the text side is faciomg down. Fold along the vertical lines

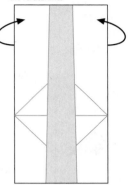

Figure 33. Step 1: Fold vertically

```perl
use constant A4 => 0;  # Change 0 to 1 if printing on A4 paper

use constant Inches2twips => 1440; # (conversion factor)

use constant Page_Width  => A4 ? 11909 : (8.5 * Inches2twips);
use constant Page_Height => A4 ? 16834 : ( 11 * Inches2twips);

use constant Smidgen     => 1/8 * Inches2twips; # fudge factor
use constant CD_Diameter => Smidgen + 4.75 * Inches2twips;
use constant Wing_Size   => (Page_Width - CD_Diameter) / 2;

use constant First_Line_Height => 40 * 10;
#----------------------------------------------------------
# Declare the two global variables:
my $out = "cd_case.rtf";
my @lines;

# The main work of the program:

get_input();
open(RTF, ">$out") or die "Can't write-open $out: $!";
doc_intro();
draw_fold_guides();
print_text();
close(RTF);
print "\nCreated $out (", -s $out, " bytes)\n";
exit;
```

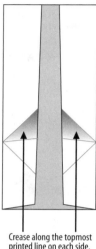

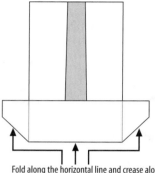

Crease along the topmost
printed line on each side.

Fold along the horizontal line and crease along
the diagonal printed lines.

Figure 34. Step 2: Crease and fold horizontally

```
#-----------------------------------------------------------

sub get_input {
  print "Enter text for CD case, then hit Enter and EOF (",
    ($^O =~ m/MSWin/) ? "control-z)\n" : "control-d)\n"
    unless @ARGV;
    # Which key you hit depends on your OS.  MSWin uses
    # control-z, whereas most everything else by default
    # uses control-d.

  @lines = <>;  # Get the input lines (either from a file,
    # or from standard input / the console)

  unless( grep m/\S/, @lines) { # if all blank
    print "\nNo input lines?  Making a blank case then.\n";
    @lines = ( '_' ); # just a dummy line
  }

  chomp(@lines); # remove the \n's
  return;
}
#-----------------------------------------------------------

sub doc_intro { # Start off the RTF file
```

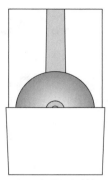

Insert the CD in the fold.

Turn over. If you want, you can crease the paper above the title line; this will make a "spine" on the CD case when it is all folded up later.

Figure 35. Step 3: Insert CD and turn over

```
    printf RTF '{\rtf1\ansi
\deff0{\fonttbl {\f0 \froman Times New Roman;}}
\paperw%s \paperh%s \deflang1033\plain\f0\fs20

{\pard\par}

', int(.5 + Page_Width), int(.5 + Page_Height);

  return;
}

#-----------------------------------------------------------

sub print_text {
  # Write the contents of @lines into this exact-positioned
  # paragraph, feeding each one through esc($line).

  printf RTF '{\pard \pvpg\phpg
\posx%s \posy%s
\absw%s \absh-%s
', map int($_ + .5), # make everything an integer

    Wing_Size + Smidgen,
    Page_Height - Page_Height * 1/4
     - CD_Diameter - First_Line_Height,
    CD_Diameter - 2 * Smidgen,
    CD_Diameter - 2 * Smidgen + First_Line_Height,
  ;
```

Turn over and crease along under the title

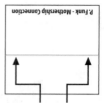

Tuck the flap between the CD
and the bottom paper edge...
you're done!!

Figure 36. Step 4: Tuck in the flap

```
    print RTF "\n\\f0\\fs20{\\fs40 ",
      # Make the first line larger
      @lines ? esc(shift @lines) : '',
      "}\n";

    foreach my $line (@lines) {
      print RTF "\n\\line ", esc($line), "\n";
    }

    print RTF "\n\\par}\n}"; # end box and document
    return;
}
#-----------------------------------------------------------

sub esc {  # return the given string, escaped as good RTF
    my $in = $_[0];
    $in =~ s{([^-"'?,\$\. _a-zA-Z0-9 ])}
            {sprintf("\\'%02x",ord($1))}eg;
    # Actually escapes much more than is necessary, but
    # doesn't handle Unicode -- see Appendix A.
    return $in;
}

#-----------------------------------------------------------

sub draw_fold_guides {  # draw all the lines!

    # draw ------- across bottom
    line(0,          Page_Height*3/4,
        Page_Width,  Page_Height*3/4 );

    # draw |   |   from top to bottom
    line(Wing_Size + Smidgen/2, 0,
        Wing_Size, Page_Height );
```

```perl
   line(Page_Width - Wing_Size - Smidgen/2, 0,
        Page_Width - Wing_Size,  Page_Height );

   # draw \   /  by the bottom line
   #      /   \
   line( Wing_Size, Page_Height*3/4,
         0, (Page_Height*3/4) + Wing_Size );
   line( Wing_Size, Page_Height*3/4,
         0, (Page_Height*3/4) - Wing_Size );
   line( Page_Width - Wing_Size, Page_Height*3/4,
         Page_Width, (Page_Height*3/4) + Wing_Size );
   line( Page_Width - Wing_Size, Page_Height*3/4,
         Page_Width, (Page_Height*3/4) - Wing_Size );
   return;
}

#-----------------------------------------------------------
# And finally, the routine that handles the grunt-work
# of actually generating the RTF code for a line from
# one page-point to another.

my $z_count; # just a counter variable

sub line {  # make a line from (x,y) to (x2,y2)
   my($x1,$y1,$x2,$y2) = map int(.5 + $_), @_;

   # Make sure we have four arguments
   use Carp;
   croak "line() takes four parameters" unless @_ == 4;

   # Get the page coordinates of northwest corner
   my $nw_x = ($x1 < $x2) ? $x1 : $x2;
   my $nw_y = ($y1 < $y2) ? $y1 : $y2;

   $x1 -= $nw_x; $x2 -= $nw_x; $y1 -= $nw_y; $y2 -= $nw_y;
   # So that (x1,y1) and (x2,y2) are relative to the NW corner

   my $w = abs($x1 - $x2); # horizontal distance
   my $h = abs($y1 - $y2); # vertical distance
   $z_count++;

   printf RTF '{*\do\dobxpage\dobypage\dodhgt%s\dpline
\dpptx%s\dppty%s \dpptx%s\dppty%s
\dpx%s\dpy%s \dpxsize%s\dpysize%s
\dplinew%s \dplinecor%s\dplinecog%s\dplinecob%s
}

', $z_count,
     $x1,$y1, $x2,$y2,
     $nw_x, $nw_y, $w, $h,
     15,  # line thickness
     0,0,0, # RGB of line color
   ;
```

```
    return;
}

__END__
```

An RTF Metadata Extractor

In the section "Document Structure" in Part I, we discussed the kinds of document metadata that could be expressed in an \info group -- such as {\author *author name(s)*} and {\title *document title*}. In this section, we consider a simple program to scan RTF documents for such metadata fields.

Suppose that the task at hand is organizing a digital library of science journal articles. We are given several thousand articles, each as an *.rtf* file with the full title in its {\title *document title*} field. We need to scan each one for its title and pass that title to another program that builds a master catalog of articles. A typical file starts with MSWord-generated RTF code like this:

```
{\rtf1\ansi\ansicpg1252\uc1 \deff27\deflang1033\deflangfe1033
{\fonttbl{\f0\froman\fcharset0\fprq2{\*\panose
02020603050405020304}Times New Roman;}{\f27\froman\fcharset0
\fprq2{\*\panose 02040502050405020303}Georgia;}}{\colortbl;
\red0\green0\blue0;\red0\green0\blue255;}{\stylesheet{\ql \li0
\ri0\widctlpar\aspalpha\aspnum\faauto\adjustright\rin0\lin0
\itap0 \f27\fs22\lang1033\langfe1033\cgrid\langnp1033
\langfenp1033 \snext0 Normal;}{\*\cs10 \additive Default
Paragraph Font;}}{\info{\title **Spectroscopic study of blue com
pact galaxies. III. Empirical population synthesis**}{\author
.}{\keywords dwarf, galaxies: evolution, galaxies: stellar con
tent, galaxies: star clusters}{\operator Xenotypo GmBH}{
\creatim\yr2003\mo6\dy11\hr2\min44}{\revtim\yr2003\mo6\dy11
\hr3\min29}{\version3}{\edmins2}{\nofpages1}{\nofwords0}
{\nofchars0}{\*\company .}{\nofcharsws0}{\vern8247}}\widowctrl
\ftnbj\aenddoc\noxlattoyen\expshrtn\noultrlspc\dntblnsbdb
```

Your program needs to extract the title from this document. In the example shown, the title is "Spectroscopic study of blue compact galaxies. III. Empirical population synthesis".

In an ideal world, MSWord would have put each bit of metadata on its own line, so that you could just grep the file for \title and see a line reading {\title Spectroscopic study

---

of blue compact galaxies. III. Empirical population synthesis}. However, MSWord, like most word processors, pays no attention to making its RTF convenient and tidy. This means that a line-based approach, as with grep, is out of the question.

However, we do have the option of reading the whole document into memory and simply looking for whatever text matches the pattern {\title...*sometext*...} -- or, as a Perl regular expression, m/\{\\title\s*([^\}]+)\}/.

A potential problem is that some of the documents contain embedded images that make the files very large. However, the \info group (containing the \title field and all other metadata) is always at the start of the document, before any document content. In theory, the parts before the \info group could be arbitrarily large; but in practice, every RTF file I've ever seen had its \info group in its first 10K -- so we need only read the first 10K of each document, rather than the whole thing.

With the regular expression m/\{\\title\s*([^\}]+)\}/s and the idea that we'll only read in the first 10K, the rest of the solution is just a matter of opening each file named on the command line and resolving any \'xx escapes in the RTF text that we match. Here is the complete program:

```perl
foreach my $in (@ARGV) {
  next unless -f $in and -r _; # Skip unreadables
  open IN, $in  or  warn( "Can't read-open $in: $!\n" ), next;
  read IN, $_, 10_000 or warn("Can't read from $in: $!\n"), next
  close(IN);
  m/^\{\\rtf/s  or  warn( "Not RTF: $in\n" ), next;

  m/\{\\title\s*([^\}]+)\}/s or warn("No title in $in\n"), next;
  print "$in: ", unesc($1), "\n";
}

sub unesc {  # resolve escapes like \'b1 for
  my $x = $_[0];
  $x =~ s/[\cm\cj]//g;  # kill meaningless newlines
  $x =~ s/\\'([a-fA-F0-9]{2})/pack("C", hex($1))/eg; # decode \'xx
  return $x;
}
```

Most of that code is actually concerned with handling rare or "impossible" errors: making sure that each *.rtf* file actually is a readable file that we really can open and read from, and that it really begins with "{\rtf". The real meat of the program is in the single line with the m/\{\\title\s*([^\}]+)\}/s, which saves the title (via the regexp parentheses) into the $1 variable that we then print.

When run on the typical RTF code we saw above, the program faithfully reports its title, here truncated just for sake of fitting on the book page:

```
% perl rtf_title.pl astro381.rtf
astro381.rtf: Spectroscopic study of blue compact galaxies...
```

Remarks on Parsing

There are some problems with the regular expression m/\{\\title\s*([^\}]+)\}/ that we use for implementing the idea of a "{\title...*sometext*...}" pattern. Our regular expression assumes that the text will contain no } characters, because the text in {\title...*text*...} must never contain formatting codes (as mentioned in Part I). So we would never run into {\title The {\i Challenger} Disaster}, but would only allow {\title The Challenger Disaster}. However, our regular expression fails to handle the case where there is a literal } expressed not as a \'7d (as I recommend in this book), but as a \} (as the RTF specification also allows).

For example, suppose we had a document called "Optimizing {N,xN} Grammars". This could be expressed as {\title Optimizing \'7bN,xN\'7d Grammars}, in which case our regular expression would match Optimizing \'7bN,xN\'7d Grammars and unesc($1) would happily return "Optimizing {N,xN} Grammars". However, it could instead have been expressed as {\title Optimizing \{N,xN\} Grammars}, in which case our regular expression would match only Optimizing \. Our approach can be salvaged for this case if we just ensure that there are no documents encoded that way, by simply looking for \{. Mercifilly, the { and } characters are rare outside of math and computer notations, so this problem is not common. (And I leave as an exercise to the reader the question of what more complicated regular expression would avoid this problem altogether by matching \{ while still stopping at {.)

But a more fundamental problem with implementing the "{\title...*sometext*...}" pattern as the regular expression m/\{\\title\s*([^\}]+)\}/ is that while it basically works for \title and other metadata fields, it is an approach that won't work for other kinds of RTF structures where formatting codes and nested groups can occur.

For example, suppose you wanted to catch the content of all footnotes in a document. After glancing at Part I's discussion of footnotes, you might try to implement this by just taking the regular expression and changing "title" to "footnote", giving m/\{\\footnote\s*([^\}]+)\}/. But consider what would happen when it meets this code:

```
{\footnote\pard\plain\chftn
: See {\i Navajo Made Easier} by Irvy Goosen}
```

Our pattern would stop matching at the first }, and so would match only \pard\plain\chftn: See {\i Navajo Made Easier while missing the rest of the content, " by Irvy Goosen". This problem cannot be solved by simply fiddling with the regular expression, because regular expressions cannot match nested patterns. We want the text up until the } matching the { that opened this group, with any number of nested {...} groups inside.

In desperation, we would have to use a real RTF parser. In my experience, there are two approaches to parsing RTF: very simple approaches which are barely more than tokenizers, and very complex approaches that compile the RTF code into document trees whose structure can represent divisions (like paragraphs and tables). That may not exactly match the group structure of the RTF document you need to parse. In both situations, whether "simple" or complex, further discussion of the parsing approaches would stop being about RTF itself, and would start being about the details of the APIs of the particular libraries available for the language you're programming in. Regrettably, this is too large a topic to explore in a book this small.

## PART IV

Reference Tables

ASCII-RTF Character Chart

Table 1 shows the main printable characters you can access in RTF, as defined by the ANSI character set (also known as Code Page 1252, which is basically Latin-1 with some characters added between 128 and 159). Accessing Unicode characters is explained in the "Character Formatting" section of Part I.

Note that while RTF escapes (\'xx) are valid for all characters, the only characters that *have* to be escaped are these three characters: {, }, and \, plus all the characters over code 127.

Table 1. ASCII-RTF character chart

ASCII code	RTF escape	Character	Character name
0–31			*Control characters; do not use*
32	\'20		Space
33	\'21	!	Exclamation mark
34	\'22	"	Double quote
35	\'23	#	Number
36	\'24	$	Dollar
37	\'25	%	Percent
38	\'26	&	Ampersand
39	\'27	'	Apostrophe
40	\'28	(	Left parenthesis
41	\'29	)	Right parenthesis

Table 1. ASCII-RTF character chart (continued)

ASCII code	RTF escape	Character	Character name
42	\'2a	*	Asterisk
43	\'2b	+	Plus sign
44	\'2c	,	Comma
45	\'2d	-	Hyphen *(use _ for nonbreaking hyphen)*
46	\'2e	.	Period
47	\'2f	/	Slash
48–57	\'30–\'39	0–9	Digits 0–9
58	\'3a	:	Colon
59	\'3b	;	Semicolon
60	\'3c	<	Less-than sign
61	\'3d	=	Equals sign
62	\'3e	>	Greater-than sign
63	\'3f	?	Question mark
64	\'40	@	Commercial at sign
65	\'41	A	
66	\'42	B	
67	\'43	C	
68	\'44	D	
69	\'45	E	
70	\'46	F	
71	\'47	G	
72	\'48	H	
73	\'49	I	
74	\'4a	J	
75	\'4b	K	
76	\'4c	L	
77	\'4d	M	
78	\'4e	N	

Table 1. ASCII-RTF character chart (continued)

ASCII code	RTF escape	Character	Character name
79	\'4f	O	
80	\'50	P	
81	\'51	Q	
82	\'52	R	
83	\'53	S	
84	\'54	T	
85	\'55	U	
86	\'56	V	
87	\'57	W	
88	\'58	X	
89	\'59	Y	
90	\'5a	Z	
91	\'5b	[	Left square bracket
92	\'5c	\	Backslash
93	\'5d	]	Right square bracket
94	\'5e	^	Caret
95	\'5f	_	Underscore
96	\'60	`	Grave accent
97	\'61	a	
98	\'62	b	
99	\'63	c	
100	\'64	d	
101	\'65	e	
102	\'66	f	
103	\'67	g	
104	\'68	h	
105	\'69	i	
106	\'6a	j	

Table 1. ASCII-RTF character chart (continued)

ASCII code	RTF escape	Character	Character name
107	\'6b	k	
108	\'6c	l	
109	\'6d	m	
110	\'6e	n	
111	\'6f	o	
112	\'70	p	
113	\'71	q	
114	\'72	r	
115	\'73	s	
116	\'74	t	
117	\'75	u	
118	\'76	v	
119	\'77	w	
120	\'78	x	
121	\'79	y	
122	\'7a	z	
123	\'7b	{	Left curly brace
124	\'7c	|	Vertical bar
125	\'7d	}	Right curly brace
126	\'7e	~	Tilde
127	\'7f		*Delete character; do not use*
128	\'80	€	Euro character
129	\'81		*Unassigned*
130	\'82	‚	Low left single quote
131	\'83	ƒ	Florin
132	\'84	„	Low left double quote
133	\'85	…	Ellipsis
134	\'86	†	Dagger

Table 1. ASCII-RTF character chart (continued)

ASCII code	RTF escape	Character	Character name
135	\'87	‡	Double dagger
136	\'88	ˆ	Circumflex
137	\'89	‰	Permil
138	\'8a	Š	S-caron
139	\'8b	‹	Single left guillemet
140	\'8c	Œ	OE-ligature
141	\'8d		*Unassigned*
142	\'8e	Ž	Z-caron
143	\'8f		*Unassigned*
144	\'90		*Unassigned*
145	\'91	'	Left single quote
146	\'92	'	Right single quote
147	\'93	"	Left double quote
148	\'94	"	Right double quote
149	\'95	•	Bullet
150	\'96	–	En dash
151	\'97	—	Em dash
152	\'98	~	Tilde
153	\'99	™	Trademark
154	\'9a	š	s-caron
155	\'9b	›	Single right guillemet
156	\'9c	œ	oe ligature
157	\'9d		*Unassigned*
158	\'9e	ž	z-caron
159	\'9f	Ÿ	Y-diaeresis
(160)	\~		Nonbreaking space
161	\'a1	¡	Inverted exclamation point
162	\'a2	¢	Cent sign

Table 1. ASCII-RTF character chart (continued)

ASCII code	RTF escape	Character	Character name
163	\'a3	£	Pound sign
164	\'a4	¤	General currency sign
165	\'a5	¥	Yen sign
166	\'a6	¦	Broken vertical bar
167	\'a7	§	Section sign
168	\'a8	¨	Spacing diaeresis
169	\'a9	©	Copyright
170	\'aa	ª	Feminine ordinal
171	\'ab	«	Left angle quotes
172	\'ac	¬	Not sign
173	\-	(-)	Soft hyphen
174	\'ae	®	Registered trademark
175	\'af	¯	Macron accent
176	\'b0	°	Degree sign
177	\'b1	±	Plus or minus sign
178	\'b2	^{2}	Superscript 2
179	\'b3	^{3}	Superscript 3
180	\'b4	´	Acute accent
181	\'b5	µ	Micro sign (Greek mu)
182	\'b6	¶	Paragraph sign
183	\'b7	•	Middle dot
184	\'b8	¸	Cedilla
185	\'b9	^{1}	Superscript 1
186	\'ba	º	Masculine ordinal
187	\'bb	»	Right angle quotes
188	\'bc	1/4	One-fourth fraction
189	\'bd	1/2	One-half fraction
190	\'be	3/4	Three-fourths fraction

Table 1. ASCII-RTF character chart (continued)

ASCII code	RTF escape	Character	Character name
191	\'bf	¿	Inverted question mark
192	\'c0	À	A-grave
193	\'c1	Á	A-acute
194	\'c2	Â	A-circumflex
195	\'c3	Ã	A-tilde
196	\'c4	Ä	A-diaeresis
197	\'c5	Å	A-ring
198	\'c6	Æ	AE-ligature
199	\'c7	Ç	C-cedilla
200	\'c8	È	E-grave
201	\'c9	É	E-acute
202	\'ca	Ê	E-circumflex
203	\'cb	Ë	E-diaeresis
204	\'cc	Ì	I-grave
205	\'cd	Í	I-acute
206	\'ce	Î	I-circumflex
207	\'cf	Ï	I-diaeresis
208	\'d0	Ð	Uppercase edh
209	\'d1	Ñ	N-tilde
210	\'d2	Ò	O-grave
211	\'d3	Ó	O-acute
212	\'d4	Ô	O-circumflex
213	\'d5	Õ	O-tilde
214	\'d6	Ö	O-diaeresis
215	\'d7	×	Multiply sign
216	\'d8	Ø	O-slash
217	\'d9	Ù	U-grave
218	\'da	Ú	U-acute

Table 1. ASCII-RTF character chart (continued)

ASCII code	RTF escape	Character	Character name
219	\'db	Û	U-circumflex
220	\'dc	Ü	U-diaeresis
221	\'dd	Ý	Y-acute
222	\'de	Þ	Uppercase thorn
223	\'df	ß	German ess-zed
224	\'e0	à	a-grave
225	\'e1	á	a-acute
226	\'e2	â	a-circumflex
227	\'e3	ã	a-tilde
228	\'e4	ä	a-diaeresis
229	\'e5	å	a-ring
230	\'e6	æ	ae-ligature
231	\'e7	ç	c-cedilla
232	\'e8	è	e-grave
233	\'e9	é	e-acute
234	\'ea	ê	e-circumflex
235	\'eb	ë	e-diaeresis
236	\'ec	ì	i-grave
237	\'ed	í	i-acute
238	\'ee	î	i-circumflex
239	\'ef	ï	i-diaeresis
240	\'f0	ð	Lowercase edh
241	\'f1	ñ	n-tilde
242	\'f2	ò	o-grave
243	\'f3	ó	o-acute
244	\'f4	ô	o-circumflex
245	\'f5	õ	o-tilde
246	\'f6	ö	o-diaeresis

Table 1. ASCII-RTF character chart (continued)

ASCII code	RTF escape	Character	Character name
247	\'f7	÷	Division sign
248	\'f8	ø	o-slash
249	\'f9	ù	u-grave
250	\'fa	ú	u-acute
251	\'fb	û	u-circumflex
252	\'fc	ü	u-diaeresis
253	\'fd	ý	y-acute
254	\'fe	þ	Lowercase thorn
255	\'ff	ÿ	y-diaeresis

RTF Language Codes

In RTF, use the \lang*thatnumber* command with the appropriate language code to label a piece of text as a particular language; for example, this paragraph in U.S. English (1033) contains a phrase in French (1036):

```
{\pard\lang1033 It had a certain
{\i\lang1036 je ne sais quoi}.\par}
```

Table 2 is a partial list of the most common language numbers. A complete list is located at *http://www.unicode.org/unicode/onlinedat/languages.html*

Note that the language values are in decimal (as used in RTF's \lang*thatnumber* command). In most Microsoft documentation, the values are (inconveniently) listed in hexadecimal.

Table 2. RTF language codes

Language name	Language code (decimal)
Not in any language	1024
Afrikaans	1078
Arabic	1025

Table 2. RTF language codes (continued)

Language name	Language code (decimal)
Catalan	1027
Chinese (Traditional)	1028
Chinese (Simplified)	2052
Czech	1029
Danish	1030
Dutch	1043
Dutch (Belgian)	2067
English (U.K.)	2057
English (U.S.)	1033
Finnish	1035
French	1036
French (Belgian)	2060
French (Canadian)	3084
French (Swiss)	4108
German	1031
German (Swiss)	2055
Greek	1032
Hebrew	1037
Hungarian	1038
Icelandic	1039
Indonesian	1057
Italian	1040
Japanese	1041
Korean	1042
Norwegian (Bokmål)	1044
Norwegian (Nynorsk)	2068
Polish	1045
Portuguese	2070

Table 2. RTF language codes (continued)

Language name	Language code (decimal)
Portuguese (Brazilian)	1046
Romanian	1048
Russian	1049
Serbo-Croatian (Cyrillic)	2074
Serbo-Croatian (Latin)	1050
Slovak	1051
Spanish (Castilian)	1034
Spanish (Mexican)	2058
Swahili	1089
Swedish	1053
Thai	1054
Turkish	1055
Vietnamese	1066

Converting to Twips

Measurements in RTF are generally in twips. A twip is a twentieth of a point, i.e., a 1,440th of an inch. It can lead to large numbers sometimes (like \li2160 to set the left indent to an inch and a half), but Table 3 should be useful for conversions. Also, see the ruler printed inside the cover of this book.

Conversions between centimeters and anything else are approximate, so figures with a preceding "~" have been rounded.

Table 3. Converting to twips

Inches	Twips	Points	Centimeters
	20 tw	1 pts	
	40 tw	2 pts	
	~57 tw		.1 cm

Table 3. Converting to twips (continued)

Inches	Twips	Points	Centimeters
	60 tw	3 pts	
	80 tw	4 pts	
1/16″	90 tw	4.5 pts	
	100 tw	5 pts	
	~113 tw		.2 cm
1/9″	160 tw	8 pts	
	~170 tw		.3 cm
1/8″	180 tw	9 pts	
1/7″	~206 tw	~10.3 pts	
	~227 tw		.4 cm
1/6″	240 tw	12 pts	
3/16″	270 tw	13.5 pts	
	~283 tw		.5 cm
1/5″	288 tw	14.4 pts	
	~340 tw		.6 cm
1/4″	360 tw	18 pts	
	~397 tw		.7 cm
	~454 tw		.8 cm
1/3″	480 tw	24 pts	
	~510 tw		.9 cm
	~567 tw		1 cm
1/2″	720 tw	36 pts	
	~850 tw		1.5 cm
3/4	1080 tw	54 pts	
	~1134 tw		2 cm
1″	1440 tw	72 pts	
	~1701 tw		3 cm
1.5″	2160 tw	108 pts	

Table 3. Converting to twips (continued)

Inches	Twips	Points	Centimeters
	~2268 tw		4 cm
	~2835 tw		˙ 5 cm
2″	2880 tw	144 pts	
	~3402 tw		6 cm
2.5″	3600 tw	180 pts	
3″	4320 tw	216 pts	
	~5669 tw		10 cm
4″	5760 tw	288 pts	
5″	7200 tw	360 pts	

Index

Other Titles Available from O'Reilly

Web Authoring and Design

HTML & XHTML: The Definitive Guide, 5th Edition

By Chuck Musciano & Bill Kennedy
5th Edition August 2002
672 pages, ISBN 0-596-00382-X

Our new edition offers web developers a better way to become HTML-fluent, by covering the language syntax, semantics, and variations in detail and demonstrating the difference between good and bad usage. Packed with examples, *HTML & XHTML: The Definitive Guide*, 5th Edition covers Netscape Navigator 6, Internet Explorer 6, HTML 4.01, XHTML 1.0, JavaScript 1.5, CSS2, Layers, and all of the features supported by the popular web browsers.

Learning Web Design

By Jennifer Niederst
1st Edition March 2001
418 pages, ISBN 0-596-00036-7

In *Learning Web Design*, Jennifer Niederst shares the knowledge she's gained from years of experience as both web designer and teacher. She starts from the very beginning—defining the Internet, the Web, browsers, and URLs—assuming no previous knowledge of how the Web works. Jennifer helps you build the solid foundation in HTML, graphics, and design principles that you need for crafting effective web pages.

Web Design in a Nutshell, 2nd Edition

By Jennifer Niederst
2nd Edition September 2001
640 pages, ISBN 0-596-00196-7

Web Design in a Nutshell contains the nitty-gritty on everything you need to know to design web pages. Written by veteran web designer Jennifer Niederst, this book provides quick access to the wide range of technologies and techniques from which web designers and authors must draw. Topics include understanding the web environment, HTML, graphics, multimedia and interactivity, and emerging technologies.

Cascading Style Sheets: The Definitive Guide

By Eric A. Meyer
1st Edition May 2000
470 pages, ISBN 1-56592-622-6

CSS is the HTML 4.0–approved method for controlling visual presentation on web pages. *Cascading Style Sheets: The Definitive Guide* offers a complete, detailed review of CSS1 properties and other aspects of CSS1. Each property is explored individually in detail with discussion of how each interacts with other properties. There is also information on how to avoid common mistakes in interpretation. This book is the first major title to cover CSS in a way that acknowledges and describes current browser support, instead of simply describing the way things work in theory.

O'REILLY®

To order: *800-998-9938* • *order@oreilly.com* • *www.oreilly.com*
Online editions of most O'Reilly titles are available by subscription at *safari.oreilly.com*
Also available at most retail and online bookstores.

The Web Design CD Bookshelf

By O'Reilly & Associates, Inc.
Version 1.0 November 2001
(Includes CD-ROM)
640 pages, ISBN 0-596-00271-8

Six best selling O'Reilly Animal Guides are now available on CD-ROM, easily accessible and searchable with your favorite web browser: *HTML & XHTML: The Definitive Guide*, 4th Edition; *ActionScript: The Definitive Guide*; *Information Architecture for the World Wide Web*; *Designing Web Audio: RealAudio, MP3, Flash, and Beatnik*; *Web Design In a Nutshell*, 2nd Edition; and *Cascading Style Sheets: The Definitive Guide*. As a bonus, you also get the new paperback version of *Web Design in a Nutshell*, 2nd Edition.

Information Architecture for the World Wide Web, 2nd Edition

By Louis Rosenfeld & Peter Morville
2nd Edition August 2002
488 pages, ISBN 0-596-00035-9

This book provides effective approaches for designers, information architects, and web site managers who are faced with sites that are becoming difficult to use and maintain. Web professionals will learn how to design web sites and intranets that support growth, management, navigation, and ease of use. This thorough introduction to the field of information architecture features updated material covering classic issues as well as new approaches to Information Architecture.

XML

XML in a Nutshell, 2nd Edition

By Elliotte Rusty Harold &
W. Scott Means
1st Edition December 2000
400 pages, ISBN 0-596-00058-8

This powerful new edition provides developers with a comprehensive guide to the rapidly evolving XML space. Serious users of XML will find topics on just about everything they need, from fundamental syntax rules, to details of DTD and XML Schema creation, to XSLT transformations, to APIs used for processing XML documents. Simply put, this is the only reference of its kind among XML books.

XSLT Cookbook

By Sal Mangano
1st Edition December 2002
670 pages, ISBN 0-596-00372-2

This book offers the definitive collection of solutions and examples that developers at any level can use immediately to solve a wide variety of XML processing issues. As with our other Cookbook titles, *XSLT Cookbook* contains code recipes for specific programming problems. But more than just a book of cut-and-paste code, *XSLT Cookbook* enables developers to build their programming skills and their understanding of XSLT through the detailed explanations provided with each recipe.

Learning XML

By Erik T. Ray with
Christopher R. Maden
1st Edition January 2001
368 pages, ISBN 0-596-00046-4

XML (Extensible Markup Language) is a flexible way to create "self-describing data"—and to share both the format and the data on the World Wide Web, intranets, and elsewhere. In *Learning XML*, the authors explain XML and its capabilities succinctly and professionally, with references to real-life projects and other cogent examples. *Learning XML* shows the purpose of XML markup itself, the CSS and XSL styling languages, and the XLink and XPointer specifications for creating rich link structures.

XML Schema

By Eric van der Vlist
1st Edition June 2002
400 pages, 0-596-00252-1

The W3C's XML Schema offers a powerful set of tools for defining acceptable XML document structures and content. While schemas are powerful, that power comes with substantial complexity. This book explains XML Schema foundations, a variety of different styles for writing schemas, simple and complex types, datatypes and facets, keys, extensibility, documentation, design choices, best practices, and limitations. Complete with references, a glossary, and examples throughout.

XSLT

By Doug Tidwell
1st Edition August 2001
473 pages, ISBN 0-596-00053-7

XSLT (Extensible Stylesheet Language Transformations) is a critical bridge between XML processing and more familiar HTML, and dominates the market for conversions between XML vocabularies. Useful as XSLT is, its complexities can be daunting. Doug Tidwell, a developer with years of XSLT experience, eases the pain by building from the basics to the more complex and powerful possibilities of XSLT, so you can jump in at your own level of expertise.

Java & XML, 2nd Edition

By Brett McLaughlin
2nd Edition September 2001
528 pages, ISBN 0-596-00197-5

New chapters on Advanced SAX, Advanced DOM, SOAP, and data binding, as well as new examples throughout, bring the second edition of *Java & XML* thoroughly up to date. Except for a concise introduction to XML basics, the book focuses entirely on using XML from Java applications. It's a worthy companion for Java developers working with XML or involved in messaging, web services, or the new peer-to-peer movement.

O'REILLY®

To order: *800-998-9938* • *order@oreilly.com* • *www.oreilly.com*
Online editions of most O'Reilly titles are available by subscription at *safari.oreilly.com*
Also available at most retail and online bookstores.

O'REILLY®

To order: *800-998-9938* • *order@oreilly.com* • *www.oreilly.com*
Online editions of most O'Reilly titles are available by subscription at *safari.oreilly.com*
Also available at most retail and online bookstores.